Twayne's United States Authors Series

EDITOR OF THIS VOLUME

Warren French

Mark Harris

TUSAS 304

photo by Jim Judkis

Mark Harris

MARK HARRIS

By NORMAN LAVERS

Arkansas State University

TWAYNE PUBLISHERS
A DIVISION OF G. K. HALL & CO., BOSTON

Library of Congress Cataloging in Publication Data

Lavers, Norman.
  Mark Harris.

  (Twayne's United States authors series ; TUSAS 304)
  Bibliography: p. 147 - 50
  Includes index.
  1.   Harris, Mark, 1922 -   —Criticism and inter-
pretation.   I.   Title.
PS3515.A757Z6   813'.5'4   77-15801
ISBN 0-8057-7209-X

For Cheryl and Gawain
and for my Mother

Contents

About the Author

Norman Lavers received the B.A. and M.A. degrees at San Francisco State College, studying with Mark Harris, Herbert Blau (founder-director of the San Francisco Actor's Workshop), Ray B. West, and Walter Van Tilburg Clark. He received the Ph.D. from the University of Iowa, where he was a member of the Iowa Writers Workshop, and held for two years one of the coveted Writers Workshop Writing Fellowships. While at Iowa, he studied and worked with critic Robert Scholes, and writers Vance Bourjaily, Kurt Vonnegut, Robert Coover, and others. He has taught at Northern Illinois University, The University of Iowa, Western Washington State College, and is currently directing the creative writing program at Arkansas State University, where in addition to his writing classes, he teaches contemporary literature, and Restoration drama. His critical articles, mainly on contemporary fiction, have appeared in such places as *College English, The University of Kansas City Review, The South Atlantic Quarterly*, and *Novel: A Forum on Fiction* and *The American Poetry Review*. He writes a regular column on recent developments in fiction for *Northeast*. His short stories have appeared in *The Ohio Review, Tri-Quarterly, Northeast*, and other little magazines. Within the past five or six years he has taken up amateur ornithology as a hobby, and though entirely self-taught, he has begun publishing photographs and technical articles on birds in such places as *The Auk*, and *Western Birds*. At the moment, between his teaching duties, and frantic bird-watching trips to the Florida Everglades, the North Pacific Ocean, and the savannahs of East Africa, he is writing a book on Restoration comedy and working on a novel.

Preface

Mark Harris has published a considerable body of work, his books have gone through several printings and reissues, and they have been widely and for the most part generously reviewed. And yet in a special way he is an unfashionable writer. Partly, I suspect, this is because he writes clearly and straightforwardly, and the deep exegetical critics of our day (producing what Leslie Fiedler has called "the higher remedial reading") prefer something crabbed, involute, and private to test their mettle on. At any rate, no other writer of comparable stature has been left so completely alone by serious criticism. John Enck interviewed him for his famous series of interviews in *Wisconsin Studies in Contemporary Literature.* Wayne Booth praised him and quoted him half a dozen times in *The Rhetoric of Fiction.* When Granville Hicks was review editor for *Saturday Review,* he used his position to boost Harris's reputation at every opportunity, and included him in his volume *The Living Novel: A Symposium.* But that is about all.

On the other hand, while the surface of Harris's works, far from being thorny and eccentric, is clear, funny, and immensely readable, his books are no more addressed to a lazy popular audience than they are to an ingenious neo-critically trained one. For he is that rarest of writers, the writer of true comedy, and comedy makes its appeal to alert intelligence. His most wonderful lines are just those a careless reader (and this includes most of his reviewers) will overlook, and the lines overlooked, the book is misread, for comic writing, to an even greater extent than other kinds, depends on its language being understood, if it is to create its greatest effect.

Of course the comedy, as all good comedy, is serious. Within the humor Harris is often asking for a radical reordering of values. Here is another way he has been unfashionable. It is difficult to assess, but it seems certain that some of his views, in particular his uncompromising pacifism, may have damaged his reputation. It is fashionable now to be a pacifist, but it was not fashionable in 1953 (*The Southpaw*) to disparage our involvement in the Korean War ("the war against Korea" Henry Wiggen keeps calling it in the novel; making me think of the gunboats in *Heart of Darkness* standing off Africa and blindly shelling the continent itself.) One reviewer, speaking as charitably as he could, thought "that Mr. Harris, like Henry, hasn't finished growing up yet."[1] Nor was it fashionable in 1957 (*Something About a Soldier*) to make heroes of the men who purposely shot off their fingers in basic training to escape combat in the Second World War, or indeed to make the sympathetic protagonist of the novel a deserter from that war. Although now this is considered one of his finest novels, at the time he had difficulty finding a publisher for it.

I do not mean here to be rising stridently to the defense of a writer whose work can defend itself. Nor do I wish to force myself into a corner from which I must assert Mark Harris is a major writer of numerous overlooked masterpieces. The books vary in quality; many are flawed one way or another. But he is a writer of intelligence and integrity and wonderful comic ability, and he has not been read, even by some of his champions, with the care that his highly controlled works deserve. He did not promise great things, and then fail miserably, inexplicably, in midcourse—that sad American trajectory. Instead he promised very good things, and he has produced them right along. Between *Trumpet to the World* in 1946 (when he was twenty-two) and *Killing Everybody* in 1973, he has so far published nine novels, three autobiographical volumes, a play, written a very successful screenplay for one of his novels, and produced a great deal of first-rate journalism and periodical writing.[2]

Mark Harris has made, is still making, his small but respectable place in modern American literature. It is certainly time his work was brought together for a first assessment.

In the first chapter I deal with those physical and personal characteristics, those biographical details, which seem to have a direct bearing on Harris's work. I particularly stress his concern with racial discrimination, his lifelong pacifism, his dislike for authority—all subsumed under his radical respect for the value of the individual as opposed to the society; also his small size, poor eyesight, and yet great interest in athletics, especially baseball; and last, his total commitment, from the very beginning, to being a writer. All these form the subjects and themes of his work.

This chapter will form the key to the following five chapters, which are critical discussions of Harris's nine novels taken up chronologically. It will be seen that in the logical (indeed almost programmatic) development of his writing career over some thirty years, Harris has not been questing about for ideas to live by, but rather, his own philosophy largely settled, he has been looking for the best formal means to embody his ideas.

In chapter seven I deal with Harris's autobiographical works. Between the writing of *Wake Up, Stupid* (1959) and *The Goy* (1970) there was a decade-long hiatus in his novel-writing, which marked a personal and artistic crisis in Harris's life. During this period he turned inward, and his major published works of this time are all strongly autobiographical, and in various ways deal with this critical period in his creative life.

In chapter eight I explain why I think Harris's significant work is all in the novel. The autobiographies are important mainly as they shed light on the novels. Although he has written some short fiction, and done a great deal of periodical writing, for the purposes of this study I have confined myself to discussing only those short works (autobiographical fragments, or writings on the craft of writing) which contributed directly to an understanding of the novels. I conclude by giving my final assessment of Harris's position as a novelist. Since Harris has been virtually ignored by serious criticism I have had to base my discussion entirely on my own careful reading of his works.

NORMAN LAVERS

Arkansas State University

Acknowledgments

I would like to thank my mother for keeping up my interest in Harris over the years; and I would like to thank my former colleague at Western Washington State College, Professor L. L. Lee, for encouraging me to undertake this study.

I would like to thank Mark Harris for reading an early draft of Chapter 1, and thereby helping me to avoid some mistakes on matters of his biography. Any mistakes which remain are of course my responsibility. I would also like to thank him for generously allowing me to quote from his published works and from letters which he wrote to me.

I also want to thank the following for permission to quote from certain material:

The Regents of the University of Wisconsin, Madison, for quotations from "Mark Harris: An Interview," by John Enck, Volume VI, Number 1 (© 1965 by the Regents of the University of Wisconsin), pp. 15 - 26;

Alfred A. Knopf, Inc., New York, for quotations from *Bang the Drum Slowly*, by Mark Harris, Copyright 1956 by Alfred A. Knopf, and *A Ticket for a Seamstitch*, by Mark Harris, Copyright 1957 by Alfred A Knopf;

The Dial Press, New York, for quotations from *The Goy*, by Mark Harris, Copyright © by Mark Harris. Reprinted by permission of the publisher, The Dial Press.

Chronology

1922   Mark Harris Finkelstein born November 19, Mt. Vernon, New York; son of Carlyle and Ruth (Klausman) Finkelstein.

1943   In army in the South, appalled at segregation and treatment of blacks.

1944   Goes AWOL, arrested, begins first novel *(Trumpet to the World)* in army hospital, discharged from army as "psychoneurotic." Joins NAACP.

1945   In St. Louis, works for International News Service, becomes involved in civil rights work, flirts with communism. Atom bomb dropped on Hiroshima. Later, in Springfield, meets "Jo," his future wife, begins collecting material for novelized biography of Vachel Lindsay *(City of Discontent)*.

1946   *Trumpet to the World.*

1948 -   Attends University of Denver, works on *The Southpaw.*
1951

1951 -   Does Ph.D. course work at University of Minnesota, and comes under the influence of pacifist Mulford Sibley.

1952   *City of Discontent.*

1953   Resident of MacDowell Colony in Peterborough, New Hampshire. *The Southpaw. Daily Worker* review praises its anti-(Korean) war sentiments.

1954   Comes to San Francisco State College as teacher.

1956   *Bang the Drum Slowly.* A story *(A Ticket for a Seamstitch)* commissioned by *Life,* but then not used. Ph.D. from University of Minnesota, under Henry Nash Smith, in American Studies. Dissertation: "Randolph Bourne: A Study in Immiscibility."

1957 -   *A Ticket for a Seamstitch. Something About a Soldier.* In
1958   Hiroshima, Japan, on Fulbright grant.

1959   *Wake Up, Stupid.* December 9, his father dies.

1961   Writes play, *Friedman & Son,* while on a Ford Foundation grant.

1962   Covers California gubernatorial race, Brown vs. Nixon, for
        Life. *Friedman & Son* produced at the San Francisco Ac-
        tor's Workshop.
1963   *Friedman & Son*.
1964   *Mark the Glove Boy*.
1964 - Attends conference in Kurashiki, Japan. Sargent Shriver
1965   calls and offers investigative job in Peace Corps, and Harris
        is investigated himself to see if he is a security risk. In
        Africa briefly on Peace Corps assignment.
1966   *Twentyone Twice*.
1967   Begins teaching at Purdue University.
1970   *The Goy*. Begins teaching at California Institute of the
        Arts.
1973   *Bang the Drum Slowly* made into movie, screenplay
        written by Harris. *Killing Everybody*. Begins teaching at
        University of Southern California.
1976   *Best Father Ever Invented* (autobiography). Begins
        teaching at University of Pittsburgh.

CHAPTER 1

"A Continual Allegory": Shaping Influences, Themes, and Credos

ANY man's story told true becomes Everyman's story: that is the assumption behind much of Mark Harris's work. In that way he justifies writing, very often, about himself, sometimes in more and sometimes in less disguised ways. His argument would be that the writer (himself, for instance) is as accurate an image as any for representing modern man.

He has never been one of those writers who denies the intimate connection between life and art. Instead the idea seems to fascinate him. He has written a biography of Vachel Lindsay *(City of Discontent)* in the form of a novel, and he has written a novel *(The Southpaw)* in the form of an autobiography. He has written about himself directly, in autobiography, and indirectly, as "the disguised person in my novels."[1] He invites us himself to play back and forth between these modes. For those interested in his life, he has suggested reading his novels.[2] Of his autobiography-in-progress he once said, "Though I don't see why anybody would be interested in my life, I do think that my experience as a writer, if honestly told, can illuminate some of the problems of being a writer in America in the middle of the 20th century."[3] In short, his fiction is a symbolical representation of himself, just as he himself is symbolical representative of The Writer, and the writer ultimately of Man. The epigraph, by Keats, Harris affixes to one of his autobiographical volumes is: "A Man's life of any worth is a continual allegory."

My intention now, and I believe it will be instructive, is to play back and forth between the two modes, the life told directly in autobiography, and indirectly in fiction. My concern throughout this chapter will be to speculate on those shaping influences in his life which have ended by shaping his art as well.

I   *The Jewish Influence*

One of the smallest influences on Harris's writing seems to be his Jewishness. Except in two works *(The Goy,* and *Friedman & Son)* he makes slight use of the Jewish milieu. A writer, of course, has no obligation to write fictions with Jewish backgrounds simply because he himself happens to be Jewish. I introduce the topic because something more complex than freedom of artistic choice seems to be operating. In 1940 Harris dropped Finkelstein from his name; and while this had a purely practical motive (at the time he could not have gotten employment otherwise), nonetheless changing one's name is a serious psychological matter. Buried within his practical reasons may have been an unconscious rejection of heritage, or even more directly of his father, with whom he appears to have had a difficult relationship.

I do not wish to exaggerate. A second reason for his choosing non-Jewish subjects may simply be that Harris left home very early, entering the army when he was barely twenty, and from then on working and going to school in different parts of the country, away from his birthplace. Thus at an early stage in his career he was away from his Jewishness, become aware of and finally obsessed by other kinds of problems. Harris's first novel is about race and has a black protagonist. His second novel expresses social concerns and is about a vagabond poet destroyed by a materialistic society. His next few novels are about coming of age and have a professional athlete for protagonist. When he came finally to write his first novel with a Jewish protagonist *(Something About a Soldier),* he was a long way from his Jewish origins, writing about a Jew a long way from *his.* The main character's Jewishness is not really an important element in the novel.[4] Not until 1962, in the play *Friedman & Son,* and then, even more directly and fully in 1970 in his novel *The Goy,* does Harris for the first time attempt to deal with Jewish characters in a "Jewish" situation. The first work we know (and the second we suspect) was written at a time of artistic and personal crisis. In each the theme is certainly "the loss of Jewish identity." The autobiographical main character in the play, Ferguson, has changed his name from his father's, Friedman, and the two are estranged. The subject of the play is their reconciliation. In the novel, the (indirectly) autobiographical protagonist is, significantly enough, the goy of the title, a Gentile attempting to become a Jew. It is not difficult to see in these works an element of guilt on the part of the author for having neglected his traditions for so long.

II The Athlete Hero

Certainly a stronger influence from Harris's early life—at least so far as his writing is concerned—is suggested by his memory, circa 1927, when he would have been five, of his father carrying him on his shoulders down the long ramps of the Polo Grounds to see the New York Giants play.[5]

For those who know of Harris chiefly through one or the other of the baseball novels (*The Southpaw, Bang the Drum Slowly, A Ticket for a Seamstitch*) that are narrated by Henry Wiggen (a six-foot three-inch 195 pound left-handed pitcher for the New York Mammoths) or through *Wake Up, Stupid,* or *The Goy,* whose protagonists, though college professors, are also powerful, superbly conditioned athletes, the first sight of Harris himself is a disappointment. He is small, slight, bespectacled. "At such occasions," he says, "I always feel fraudulent, as if I have misrepresented myself: people greet me with obvious disappointment, under the impression, I know, that I am seven feet tall and heroically athletic, as I wish I were. Failing of this, I write as a compensation for Nature's negligence."[6]

The motif of the athlete hero in books by so unathletic an author is worth examining. Is it, as Harris not altogether seriously suggests, simple wish fulfillment? We remember that the creators of the Superman comic strip were two puny kids who were beaten up by all their classmates. I suspect there may be something to this, but there is more to the matter. Henry Wiggen, though a fine athlete and smart enough in his way, is semiliterate, hardly an intellectual. If Henry is an indirectly autobiographical "disguise" for Harris, then the brawn instead of brain is the disguise, the sort of trade-off more obvious writers make when they make their protagonist a painter or sculptor. Henry has a talent, exploits it, works hard, gets or makes some breaks, and becomes successful at what he is doing—and discovers that he has defined himself as a man in the process. A writer does the same. Any man's life is Everyman's life.

Lee Youngdahl in *Wake Up, Stupid,* and Westrum in *The Goy,* are more complex. With them, brain and brawn are combined. They are no longer simply the author disguised: they are the author magnified. But we are still not back to simple wish-fulfillment, for they are also both men at war with themselves. The very greatness of their gifts (they are also physically attractive to women) leaves them dissatisfied with their lives. Whatever they do is not quite enough, does not use them quite fully. What they come back to at the end is a kind of satisfaction with what they have, and what they have—a nice wife and family, a reasonably satisfying teaching job, better than moderate success in their professional life, better friends than they at first thought—are all the things, it turns out, they would have had without the fine physique and handsome appearance. They have learned to value what Harris himself, one suspects, has learned, or is trying to learn, to value. They have simply had more options to cross off before finding satisfaction. It is not the author, therefore, but the dissatisfaction which has been magnified.

III   *Army-training in the South*

The strongest shaping forces on Harris appear to have been his experiences in the army. Not only did he actually begin his writing career at this time, but here can be found the genesis of the themes and images that would continue forever after to occur in his writing.

In 1943, as a sheltered young man from upstate New York, he came to Georgia for basic training. We know from his own statements that before he could be sent overseas he had gone AWOL, been arrested and put in the stockade, and was finally discharged from the army as a "psychoneurotic."[7]

Harris tells us to go to his novel *Something About a Soldier* to find out what happened. In this novel, the hero, Jacob Epstein, a young boy very much like Harris must have been at the time, undergoes all of these experiences, in a way that closely parallels Harris's own. Jacob is filled with guilt and shame for what he has done, but the novel makes it clear that he has, not altogether knowingly, done the sane, intelligent thing, that the boys who quietly permitted themselves to be taught to kill, and then allowed themselves to be shipped off to certain death, were the ones behaving irrationally. Such a moral works very well as fable, however defensive it may tend to sound as autobiography.

At any rate, what is certain is that Harris was left with an indelible sense of the absurdity of war, even this war against Hitler, which as a Jew he might have felt justified in supporting. Ultimately he became an uncompromising pacifist. A major event for him during the period, a sort of focus for his feelings, the point from which many of his chronologies begin, was the dropping of the atom bomb on Hiroshima. When, over a decade later, he received a Fulbright grant to teach abroad, it was to that Japanese city he took himself and his family.

In Georgia he also became aware for the first time of the treatment of blacks in the United States, with segregation in the society and in the army itself. He reacted to the racial situation as to a part of the total absurdity. He wrote, angrily, a first novel about race, a novel which he feels now that he spoiled because of the axes he had to grind. But the question of racial discrimination, just as his pacifism, continues to recur in his writing.

IV   *"I Write, I Think, of Persons, Not of*
Crowds": Authority and the Individual

It is evident that in his personal life Harris has sided, and outspokenly sided, against authority. He demonstrated for the Rosenbergs, for Chessman, against the House Un-American Activities Committee, signed a public statement supporting the Free Speech movement at Berkeley, rebelled against army discipline, and so on. The difficulty is in telling to what extent his opposition to authority is Oedipal reflex (his boss at San Francisco State accused him of being a "boss hater"[8]) and to what extent the positions he has taken are simply the reasoned positions which would be taken by any man of goodwill. Harris himself suggests that there may be something conditioned in his response. "In politics I usually oppose the incumbency, recoil from prevailing tastes, and find myself unable to affiliate in spirit or even in fact with any power bloc larger than the company of a few friends." But he quickly cautions us against making him too extreme a rebel, too rabidly anti-establishment. After all, he says, "My books have regularly been published by capitalists and read by Philistines."[9]

What is relevant, it seems to me, is how seldom opposition to authority, as such, is an important factor in his novels. In the novels it is not so much that power is opposed as that the underdog is championed, which is a fine distinction, I know, but is the shade I am after. What is opposed is not a known boss, but "government," "society," "the war machine"—any faceless, impersonal monolith which can exert pressure on the sacred individual. It is the known, personal, nonabstract individual whom Harris cares about, the larger abstraction of any kind that he distrusts. Championing the underdog, he had flirted in 1944 - 45 with communism, but discovered—to judge by Jacob's experience in *Something About a Soldier*—that communism was itself just another of those abstractions which would make the individual a pawn in its service.

At this point, then, the opposition to authority dovetails with his pacifism, and with his concern for civil rights. It is faceless authority which, ignoring the value of the unique individual, lumps all young men together and sends them off to kill or be killed. It is faceless authority which, ignoring the value of the unique individual, lumps all with black skins together and denies them opportunity.

V   *The Dedication to Writing*

Lee Youngdahl, the protagonist of *Wake Up, Stupid,* at the beginning of the novel has just completed a long play and now begins writing letters to all his friends. He also proposes keeping a journal—just to keep his hand in, just so he can do a little writing every day, as a boxer punches the bag a little every day.

The practice and the attitude are very much autobiographical. Since the time Harris began his first novel, twenty years old, lying in an army hospital waiting for his discharge ("I never had it so good"),[10] he has considered himself to be a writer before all else. That first book finished *(Trumpet to the World)*, he immediately set out "in quest" of the second.[11] And this has been his regular practice, with the result that a major work has appeared, on the average, every two or three years for the past thirty years. And when a major work was not underway, he kept his hand in with other kinds of writing. For instance, in addition to his great output of books and articles, Harris can casually mention, in 1965, that he is on page 389 of his autobiography and page 11,000 of his journal![12]

He has always taken it for granted, however, that to write the kind of books he wants to write, he would need to support himself by doing some other sort of work. In the mid-1950's I was a student in his creative-writing class at San Francisco State, and I remember his giving the class occasional lectures on the economics of being a writer. "Read *Walden* at least once a year," was his first injunction. Thoreau's theory was not to aim at making a great deal of money, but rather to aim at requiring very little, so that the minimum amount of time is used in getting it. There was nothing worse, Thoreau thought, than to see a man devote his whole life to getting a living. The problem with that, Harris would add, is that it left him no time for writing.

Harris's own early experiences leading the Thoreauvian life led him to a number of temporary jobs in journalism, and once to ghost-writing a book on photo-retouching. But, married and soon with children to support, Harris got a higher degree, and with the

majority of serious writers in mid-twentieth-century America, turned to teaching. This has not, to judge by comments in his novels
and autobiographical writing, been the perfect solution, but no
solution is perfect, and by and large, it appears to have been at least
the best solution:

> I would certainly react against people—certain kinds of writers, es-
> pecially—who deplore the universities. They say it ruins you and so forth.
> Well, it seems to me many other occupations are much more hazardous for
> a writer. At best a university is a place in which the individual will extend
> his intelligence. This is not an atmosphere of, let's say, a newspaper office,
> or a day laborer, or a railroad worker, or business office; and in that sense I
> think the university is certainly the best place. One of the things a universi-
> ty includes is the idea of extending independent thought that may even
> mean conflict with the university, and the university will not only keep him
> but perhaps even value him. This is not true of an insurance office. I also
> think that the writer must keep himself as a writer separate from himself as
> a scholar or analyst or at least make the atmosphere work for him, if he can.
> It is not easy, but then writing well is not easy in any environment.[13]

VI   *"I Write. Let the Reader Learn to Read":*
 Purity of Style, Content, Form

Harris's artistic credos have altered over time, as he has altered.
But along with change there have been certain constants. The most
important of these is the Jamesian tenet to dramatize, to show clearly for the perceptive reader, but never to explain for the lazy one. "I
shall not tell you anything. I shall allow you to eavesdrop on my
people, and sometimes they will tell the truth and sometimes they
will lie, and you must determine for yourself when they are doing
which. You do this every day. Your butcher says, 'This is the best,'
and you reply, 'That's *you* saying it.' Shall my people be less the
captive of their desires than your butcher?"[14]
He had a frustrating but instructive encounter with *Life* when
that magazine commissioned him to write a Henry Wiggen story for
them. At first he had held back a bit, worried that this or that aspect
of the story might be too controversial for a mass-circulation
magazine. But the associate editors told him he was mistaken, told
him to open up and write what he wanted. He did so, but the
resulting story (published later as *A Ticket for a Seamstitch*) was
finally turned down by the editor-in-chief, who published in place
of it a shoddy piece of book-of-the-month-club writing.[15]

I see at last a chief difficulty of American fiction: I see that a magazine like *Life* objects less to controversial subject matter than to difficult style. Not irreverence, but craftsmanship, dismays the editors of mass media. There is easy reading. And there is literature. There are easy writers, and there are writers. There are people whose ears have never grown, or have fallen off, or have merely lost the power to listen. And there are people with ears.[16]

Lee Youngdahl in *Wake Up, Stupid* has the same instructive experience with commercial literature when he tries to have his play produced on Broadway. A "play doctor" is brought forth to make his play easier to understand. It is a defining experience for Youngdahl, who withdraws his play and his chance for wealth. As Harris put it, when his story was rejected by *Life*, "In a twinkling was a small fortune lost. Had I ever really counted upon it in the first place, and begun to live the life of a man worth fifty cents a word, I would have been in serious difficulty with myself and with my art."[1]

Another constant is Harris's concern with the prose itself. As might be expected of a writer who tries to write every day, who virtually trains as an athlete trains, he considers perfection of style very important. But style so practiced becomes reflex, becomes instinctive, has no further need of self-consciousness.

I think this must be true in athletics; somebody just knows he is having a good day. Later, it is always a joke: the baseball player returns to the clubhouse, the sports writers run up to the winning pitcher and they say, "How come you did so well? What pitch did you throw to so-and-so in the eighth inning?" The pitcher can't remember what he threw, but he just knew he threw the right one. It all came out of the feeling, the motion, the rhythm. . . . I don't mean to say that the writer is mindless. After one has been writing for some time perhaps he loses more and more terminology and more and more trusts to feeling.[18]

Certain of his credos are shifting or developing in time. He speaks of "moving more toward formal writing. . . . I find myself more interested in, more responsive to, in my own work, the more formal kinds of good English writing. When I was a student I rebelled against this. The baseball books are written out of a rebellion against formal language."

I think the problem is, as one grows older, that the things he has to say cannot be said by a semi-literate narrator. This is why somebody along the way invented the English language, the Anglo-Saxon tradition. Some people had some rather high-minded things to say in law and history and biography and fiction and poetry, and we arrived at a specific language, a grammatical English. I don't mean only grammatical, I mean stately English, good English. . . . For what I know now I simply need a fuller English.[19]

Harris expresses a desire to achieve, or move toward, purity in content as well as language. "When I was young I wrote novels of abstract ire about Negroes and young rebels, but now I see that what matters is how well you write, how truly, not what you write about, not timeliness or topicality."[20] The movement here, to use Stephen Dedalus's familiar terms, is from "kinesis" to "stasis."

Harris is conscious of another kind of movement, toward purity in his writing, purity of what might be called *form*. John Enck, interviewing him in 1965, asks,

> *Have you moved with your narrator's perception from Henry Wiggen to Lee Youngdahl, and now to yourself, in* Mark the Glove Boy? *Is this a last step or is there another one?*
> Well, if I have moved finally as I have to the "I," I would hope that the "I" becomes increasingly perceptive. The "I" may always appear. It may be under other names in future works but I would hope that I always choose such work or such a viewpoint in such a way as to make the fullest possible use of myself.
> *You commented about a kind of pure fiction as a removing of yourself. If one can speak of this matter in stages, would something like that be a next stage?*
> Though I wouldn't like to commit myself to any further development, I would imagine something like that may happen. Yes, I would finally be through with myself as the disguised person in my books and then move into a pure form of either fiction or non-fiction.[21]

In his most recent novel, *Killing Everybody*, it seems to me Harris takes this last step. Among other things, in the following survey of his novels I shall attempt to demonstrate how the various disguises and permutations of the self ultimately displace themselves into pure form, how the logical culmination of writing about the self seems to be, finally, to achieve the absence of self.

CHAPTER 2

"Novels of Abstract Ire":
Trumpet to the World,
and City of Discontent

H ARRIS'S third book, *The Southpaw*, with its baseball setting, was his first popular success and also his first fully mature novel. It was, in short, Harris's entry into the major leagues. Since, like most writers, Harris is constantly rifling his own life history to use in his fictions, it is tempting to see an autobiographical element in that book when Henry Wiggen, the baseball-player protagonist, spends two summers in the minor leagues, where he shook off his "greenness and was getting ready to go up to the big-time."

Harris's first two novels, *Trumpet to the World* (1946) and *City of Discontent* (1952), display, as Harris is the first to admit, a certain amount of greenness. They were strongly thesis oriented, which perhaps is not a fault unless the thesis twists the novel away from its own truth. But it is a fact that these novels occasionally followed truth of concept rather than their own inner logic, and it is for this reason Harris later called them novels of "abstract ire."

I   Trumpet to the World

Willie Jim has no official birth date, no last name. He is black, born in a packing-crate hovel in a thicket in rural Georgia. On the day he is born his father is killed, victim of some white man's aimless violence. His mother, faced with the task of feeding too many mouths, tries to drown him. But he struggles and thwarts her, for even then his character is stamped as one who will battle fiercely against all odds, and she lets him live.

He has a strong, inquiring mind as well as a strong body, and while still very young sets out barefoot, illiterate, more than anything else a young animal, down the road to the nearest city. He is so ignorant that he actually walks upright like a white man, instead of stooping humbly like a nigger. Starving, delirious, he is soon beaten senseless and thrown into jail.

When he is released, he gets a job sweeping out a colored restaurant and begins learning very quickly about city life, shoes, money, and about women (he is so big he looks like a grown man, rather than barely seventeen). He also begins teaching himself how to read. Hardest of all for him is to learn that blacks are considered inferior to whites and cannot have the same opportunities, such as access to good schools, to the university, to the library with its shelves of books going idle. His pride and his hunger to learn are both great, and frustration builds up in him as he sees completely incomprehensible obstacles put in his way merely because of the color of his skin.

His first boyish act of rebellion is to take the money carefully saved from his job and buy a gold suit, an orange tie, purple socks, and go stalking about the streets of the city glaring at whites, refusing to give way for them on the streets. He is looking for a collision, but no one quite dares challenge this big, aggressive man.

Soon such behavior begins to seem futile to Willie Jim, and he sets out walking once more, this time heading North, where everything will be different. However, as he goes, the last words he had heard from his boss at the restaurant, a black man who knew enough more than his fellows that he had been nicknamed "professor," begin to sink in and make sense to him. Willie Jim had said:

" 'Fesser, you been North and South and East and West, you say. What's it like North?" and Professor Williams said impressively that it was much different in the North.

Willie Jim wanted to hear more, more about the North, and the professor decided to temper his tale with truth. "In the North you ain't nowhere," he said, confusingly. "In the North you go to two colleges and then you carry bags at the railroad station."

"You go to college together?"

"Together?"

"Colored with white?"

"If you wants," the professor said. "But in the South you ain't nowhere, yet you somewhere" (pp. 51 - 52).[1]

Eddie Mae picks him up hitchhiking. She is a white girl, daughter of a red-neck Georgian, a retired colonel. But her father has just died, and she is on her own in the big family house. She knows her father's views were wrong, but it is hard for her to go completely against her upbringing. She takes Willie Jim into her house, and begins educating him, giving him harder and harder books to read. Partly she is fighting with herself, trying to make herself see him as an equal. And he must fight too, for he has learned distrust of whites. At length he begins to pass her up in knowledge, and, though they are still full of misgivings, she takes him into her bed.

He begins writing poetry, and almost immediately starts publishing, and even starts to develop a small reputation. He becomes politically active, and tries to organize the blacks working in menial jobs nearby to strike for better conditions ("Never get respeck till we respeck ourselves"—p. 76), but here he is a failure. The cowed workers crawl abjectly back to work at the first glance from their overseers.

When Eddie Mae becomes pregnant, she moves up to liberal New York City to avoid the dangers of having a half-black child in Georgia. Willie, remembering the professor's words, stays behind in Georgia, where he can continue fighting for his people. He begins writing a book, which will "trumpet to the world" the black man's situation. He is twenty-one when he finishes the book (the age Harris was when finishing this book), but somehow in the course of writing it he has written out his bitterness. He begins to feel the race situation really no longer exists. With the Second World War underway, he goes down to a building where blacks and whites together are donating their blood. Eddie Mae sells her father's house, and with the money they now have, Willie Jim buys another nice house in Georgia, fixes it up for his one-day returning wife (as he considers Eddie) and child.

He awakens in terror, his house in flames, white men shouting curses at him. He flees naked into the night, starves, freezes, and at last, at the point of death, is taken in by a poor family of blacks. He will never again forget his blackness.

With all his papers lost in the fire (not to mention his novel manuscript), he is soon arrested and given the choice of going to jail or joining the army.

A new stage of his life begins in the army, for, though he is segregated into a black detachment, morale is high, and he and the others strive to be the best soldiers possible, ready to go overseas and fight for their country. Things will be different, they believe, when the war is over and the whites realize how valiantly the blacks fought. And Willie Jim will be the most valiant among them.

Once more he has forgotten his blackness, and once more he is reminded of it. Rather than being sent over to fight, the blacks, after training to a fine edge of combat readiness, are all sent to be janitors at stateside army camps. Disheartened, Willie strikes back, goes AWOL, is thrown into the stockade. He serves his time, and when he gets out, a wise and humane company commander sees his potential and helps him set up a school to teach reading and writing to the many illiterates, black and white, on the army post. The school succeeds brilliantly, and Willie Jim feels he has found himself.

Once more he has forgotten and still once more he is reminded. The company commander is transferred; the new red-neck company commander immediately calls a halt to the school, and in a violent confrontation strikes Willie, who strikes back, gravely injuring him.

Willie runs. He joins his wife in New York and they hide themselves in the city. But by now his new book has been published, and suddenly he has friends and supporters all around the country, lawyers offering him service, even white soldiers offering to testify that they saw the company commander strike first. The novel ends at this point, on a note of both hope and irony: "Willie Jim's book would be translated and men would read, digest his words, in the language of another people, and they, too, would look to Georgia in a place called America. They would wonder that this strange story was written in the land that sang, freedom" (p. 242).

II   *Black and White*

Where the novel falls down, it seems to me, is in a certain simplifying of outline, a certain reduction of human complexity. The Southern whites remain at the level of comic stereotype: "[Willie Jim] drives like he owns the highway. No more respect for white folks than if he was in New York or some such place. Seems like it ain't a free country no more" (p. 101). On the other hand, the New York Northerners Eddie Mae meets are breathtakingly liberal, uncomplicatedly relating to people of all races and creeds. Willie Jim himself takes baths and showers more often than any other character I can think of in literature. Only Eddie Mae, with her

Southern upbringing, is at all ambivalent, briefly afraid that Willie
Jim will be funny-smelling or turn out to be a black superstud in
bed—but luckily, apparently, he is neither.[2]

But this first novel, written by a very youthful Harris, already has
many of the qualities of the later books. The narrative is strong and
sustained, following its repeated, constantly widening pattern of
trust and betrayal. Characters, however briefly sketched, come to
life for us—from Rilla, at the beginning of the book, Willie Jim's
mother, honest and innocent in her wilderness, to the sallow man,
near the end, who is beaten up in the stockade for saying some
Negroes might be as good as some whites. Willie Jim is a powerful
and convincing, if finally a rather two-dimensional character. Eddie
Mae may be the slightest character in the novel, but Harris
throughout his career has had trouble creating female characters.
The prose, where it flashes, already shows promise of the fine stylist
to come:

> The state of Georgia has been called a red ocean of islands.
> The color is chosen from the soil which, wherever exposed, is a bright,
> rich crimson.
> The islands can be only tiny Southern towns, separated and connected by
> a network of never-ending highways. Here and there are larger islands:
> Atlanta, Savannah, Columbus, Augusta.
> And on the high seas, off the trade routes, exist still smaller, uncon-
> sidered islands, unseen by the swift traffic that flows between the
> mainlands; minor islands, ignored by the census taker, the schoolmaster,
> the churchman and the charities, the poller of public opinion (p. 3).

III   City of Discontent

When *City of Discontent* (1952) was reprinted in 1963, Harris
wrote an introduction for the new edition in which he quite candidly disparaged this early work. "My book was . . . published, not in
haste, but perhaps too soon. On the other hand, how could I have
put it indefinitely off? A writer must discharge his mistakes and go
on to others." And though he admits he has not quite banished the
book from his shelves "my own volume, like some aged, wasting,
distant cousin occupies a sentimental place in the house without
contributing to the family's present style."[3] This is just, and yet too
harsh. The book has its weaknesses, but it also has a power and
authority which keep this oddly hybrid work, a novelized biography
of Vachel Lindsay, fresh and alive in a way that a more documen-
tary treatment of its subject and its time might not have done.

The book opens with a solidly written recreation of history: Springfield, Illinois, at the time of Lindsay's birth in 1879. Lindsay grows up to be not quite the son his father wanted, not a doctor like him, a practical man, but rather a dreamer, a poet. When Vachel is eighteen, he hears William Jennings Bryan, the magnificent orator, and for a moment there is a new spirit of liberalism in the land, of care for the wretched and dispossessed, for values beyond mere buying and selling.[4] This new spirit fades quickly but not before it has set the direction of Lindsay's life.

He flunks out of medical school. His father, saddened but generous, allows him to go to the Chicago Art Institute to study painting. Here "he knows for the first time that art has something to do with money and money has something to do with art. Not much, but something" (p. 77). He and his artist friends are soon penniless and starving, some selling out to Mammon and becoming hacks, others refusing to sell out. One girl becomes an actual prostitute to save herself from having to prostitute her art. Vachel goes off to New York and sells poems on the street two for a nickel—anything to keep alive.

Then, with a vision of himself as a wandering troubadour, an enemy of Mammon, he goes vagabonding on foot across the nation, taking his poems door to door to the people. He will not accept money but reads his poems to lonely farmers in exchange for food and a place to sleep the night.

When at last, weary and blistered, he returns home, he has been absent twelve years. He is thirty. He has amounted to nothing. And yet, when he had been on the road, one out of two people had opened their doors for him, and he believes—in spite of considerable contrary evidence—that men are good.

He takes various jobs, but they leave him too weary to write poetry at night, and he realizes this is part of Mammon's conspiracy to silence him. He then tries, but without success, to make money with his poetry. In the meantime he begins meeting like-minded, socialist-leaning people in Springfield. They support Debs for President, and, in the great athletic event of the period, favor Jack Johnson, the black fighter, over Jim Jeffries, a white man. Vachel and his friends feel the people, in their own way, are pushing to make things better:

The people unburdened themselves of a king, and in time they overthrew slavery, and along the way they taught themselves to read and write, and they reduced the length of the working day, and they took children from the factories and sent them into red-brick schoolhouses, and they do not lynch or riot as much as they once did, and they do not pass the death sentence so often or imprison the insane any longer . . . seeing sooner or later through the mist of words and deception, sifting true from false and right from wrong (p. 161).

He takes off vagabonding again, older and wiser on this trip. He sees poverty and misery and combats it in the only way he knows how, trying to vanquish indifference and Mammon with songs "preaching a gospel of beauty" (p. 168). "Maybe it will never be poetry for the ages, but at least it will be poetry for now and help people here and now to improve their world" (p. 168). He begins to see virtues in his drifting, his refusal to be broken by the system: "beggary is an act of defiance and revolt" (p. 169). He gets an idea for a folk poetry, "and maybe if a poet really wants to get something across to people he must keep himself in check and not deal in special, vague and mystical things; he must try to see as other people see, and he must at the same time be just one short step ahead of the people, not two or three or half a dozen because the people move ahead just one short step at a time" (p. 179). "The goal is not great poetry but a great humankind" (p. 180).

During this period a momentous thing has happened. Harriet Monroe rents a small office on Cass Street in Chicago and founds *Poetry: A Magazine of Verse*. A literary revival begins. Vachel Lindsay writes his poem "General William Booth Enters into Heaven." He is discovered, published, begins to make his reputation. And then, not a failure this time, with a sense of accomplishment, he returns home.

"In all, there are six books in the four good years, beginning with the time of Booth and ending with the time of war when all the forward upward motion stops, when the building and the softening and the deepening cease and the documents no longer matter" (p. 197). The First World War, and Wilson throws Bryan, a pacifist, out of his cabinet, and Debs, the socialist, is arrested. "The whole liberal movement which had risen so proudly under Bryan, Theodore Roosevelt, and La Follette, was tired. The spirit of the liberals was bewildered" (p. 235). Admirals and generals run the government with Wilson, the free press goes under, and it is not a time for poets. Vachel is a pacifist, and everyone cuts him now.

Is he mad to be a pacifist at this time? he asks himself. No, those fighting the war are mad. Has the world been made safe for democracy?

When the war ends, the poets have all gone into retreat, living in small enclaves in New York or Chicago or Santa Fe. They have become obscure, writing for one another only, turning from the people:

The rout is complete, and the hundreds who never threatened to be great follow the leaders [T. S. Eliot and Ezra Pound] and wave the same banners from the rails of sailing ships: Down with the Heart, Let the Brain Rule. To Hell with Babbitt.⁵ He is not Worth Saving. Down with the History Book, Up with the Greek. Away with the Simple Word, Give us a Good Old-Fashioned fourteenletter word in Greek or Chinese if Possible that Nobody Can Understand and Nobody Will Want to Understand. Babbitt is not Worth Saving (p. 273).

Vachel, once more alone, goes on a series of exhausting tours, reading his poetry in almost every town and city in the country, still believing that Babbitt must be saved if the country is to be saved.

He is a man to be reckoned with. . . . He will be deceived once. And he will be fooled a second time. And if the times are right he will lose his way a third time because George is not a fast thinker or a deep reader. He is a plodder. He is a foot soldier. He will march behind evil men in a first war and in a second war. But he will not go marching and dying forever. It may take disaster to awaken him, but somewhere along the way he will indeed awaken. And you [the poets]—must bring him awake" (p. 288).

In the end the tours break his health. "Who in hell appointed you to save the world?" (p. 285) his friends ask him, begging him to rest and write new poems. But he continues. He has a wife and children now to support, and the tours barely bring in enough for them to exist. In the end it has been one more trap by Mammon, keeping him silent. The people have let him down, coming to hear him chant once more "The Congo," but not listening, not buying the books.

A broken man, he goes home a last time, unable to think, unable to write, and at the age of fifty-two takes poison and dies.

IV   *The Important Thing*

"The thing about my poetry," Vachel says, "is this: the sermon and the proclamation are the important thing" (p. 210). We may take this to have been, at the time of writing, Harris's own view, for he recanted it later, in words I have already quoted: "When I was a young man . . . I wrote novels of abstract ire about Negroes and young rebels, but now I see that what matters is how well you write, how truly, not what you write about, not timeliness or topicality."[6]

I think Harris accurately pinpoints the book's weakness. His later works are certainly not devoid of thesis; *Something About a Soldier* (1957), for instance, and even his latest, *Killing Everybody* (1973), are both outspokenly pacifistic, and yet with both of these, the fable comes first, and as in all true art, the thesis, however seriously intended, ends up being an excuse for the fable, rather than the other way around.

The problem perhaps is that Harris chose to work with a real man living in a real time to illustrate his thesis, and when this real man's history did not quite coincide with the thesis, something had to bend. If the sermon is what is most important, then it is truth to the man's life which must be sacrificed. This is not entirely a problem special to writing biography, for even a fictional character begins to develop his own truth, which cannot safely be falsified—but the actual person is even more recalcitrant, for when the author sees him bending the wrong way, he cannot go back and rewrite his early life, to make him come out differently.

The book might have been more successful if its purpose had been merely to explore Lindsay as a very complex personality, a man emotionally crippled by a too-indulgent, too-close mother, a too-remote, too-severe father—the familiar Oedipal beginning, which can work itself out in so many different ways. Perhaps Vachel *had* to put all his energy and ambition into his irregular job of troubadour because an inability to accept his father made him rebel against regular kinds of work; perhaps he *had* to have his love affair with humanity at large, since his closeness to his mother forbade closeness to another woman. A fallible human being, in short, coping as best he can, trying to turn his hurts and hindrances into positive achievement. He succeeds for awhile. But the balance is too difficult to maintain to the end, and begins to crumble as he grows older, loses his mother, and begins chasing the young girls he had missed chasing when he was their age. He marries one finally, but too late, perhaps, for he no longer seems able to function as a writer.

Harris later realized that he had been too simplistic, seeing everything in social or political, rather than psychological, terms. In his introduction to the 1963 edition he quotes the first biographer of Lindsay, Edgar Lee Masters, as saying that a pension would have left Lindsay happy and fruitful in his old age, but Harris seems to doubt it himself, seems to see Lindsay's private destiny working itself out despite the immediate social background: "He who had once marched with Booth on a dollar a day could not now live on ten thousand a year" (Introduction).

But in the book he does not say this. In the book it is society doing it, the world growing steadily more crass and vulgar, getting and spending, laying waste everyone's power. The attachment to his mother, since it cannot be altogether ignored, has a few scant, isolated paragraphs devoted to it; the escapades with young students, the turn to anti-Semitism, the possible domestic sordidness of his last years—all delicately, almost charmingly, skipped around, the system blamed for all.

V   *Final Assessment*

But these faults can easily be overstressed. The book is in many ways a remarkable performance. The breadth of knowledge and experience revealed is astonishing in a book by so young a man. The social and historical background essential to the work is re-created for us vividly and convincingly, if sometimes the techniques Harris employs are a little too reminiscent of the newsreels and biographies of John Dos Pasos's *U. S. A.* trilogy. But unlike that work, Harris's book does not show its age. It remains fresh and very readable (just as I found Lindsay's poems, picking them up again for the first time in years, surprisingly vital). The secret, I think, is in the immense authority of the prose, a virtuoso performance which almost singlehandedly sustains the entire structure with its certainty and boldness. Oddly, with this richness at his disposal, Harris in his next three novels stopped writing in his own voice, and adopted instead the limited vocabulary of a partially educated professional athlete. Perhaps it was good discipline, for with the fine prose so readily available to him, he might at length have let sheer stylistic brilliance overwhelm every other consideration. Perhaps tying his hands in this way in his next few books forced him to give proper attention to the development of full characters, to the interlocking of narrative and theme, so that when once again he unstopped his organ, it was with the certainty that he also had behind him the full resources of a mature novelist.

CHAPTER 3

"In the Henry Wiggen Manner": The Southpaw, Bang the Drum Slowly, *and* A Ticket for a Seamstitch

M ARK Harris has written three "baseball" novels, all narrated by Henry Wiggen, a left-handed pitcher for the New York Mammoths. The three, *The Southpaw* (1953), *Bang the Drum Slowly* (1956), and *A Ticket for a Seamstitch* (1957), form a sort of loose trilogy, with Wiggen a green rookie in the first, a maturing professional in the second (now nicknamed "Author" Wiggen by the other players), and a matured veteran in the third. The books are linked by the developing character of Wiggen, by the baseball setting, and by the fact that a number of characters recur, but they do not form a trilogy in the sense of being thematically unified, or of depending one upon the other, or of having been, from the beginning, planned as a trilogy. In fact it is evident that each book was written as it came, with no particular thought of the volume to follow.

The books show a great advance over the earlier novels, show indeed the fulfillment of the earlier promise. The improvements are especially in the management of plot, the unity of structure and theme. But the novels offer a special problem.

Henry James tells us we must let the author choose his subject and judge him only on how well he handles it. But there are subjects *and* subjects. A pawnbroker, the owner of a tiny grocery store, even a college professor can be the hero of a serious novel, and no one raises an eyebrow. But a book about cowboys or gangsters or baseball players needs to explain itself. At the beginning of this chapter I had to put the word "baseball" in quotation marks, to show the novels are not *about* baseball. The reason is that the

34

glamorous subjects have too often been falsely glamorized for pop- ular consumption. This does not mean they cannot be used for the purposes of serious literature. The sophisticated reader knows better than to condemn all "westerns" lest he miss Walter Van Tilburg Clark's *Ox-Bow Incident,* or Don Berry's *Trask;* all "thrillers" lest he miss John Hawkes's *The Lime Twig;* all "baseball" novels lest he miss Bernard Malamud's *The Natural,* or Robert Coover's *Universal Baseball Association.* But there is initial suspicion, and the subject must be justified; the quotation marks must be earned.

Harris himself has often, and perhaps a bit defensively, tried to "locate" these novels. In the essay "Easy Does It Not" he presents an imaginary dialogue between himself and his bemused readers:

> They say, I cannot understand your book. I think you left something out.
> But everything is there. Everything you need to know is there.
> I am told, It has baseball players in it.
> Yes.
> Then it is about baseball.
> No. (pp. 116 - 17).

He reiterates this with the epigraph (from Wright Morris's *The Huge Season)* to *Bang the Drum Slowly:*

> He wiped his face with the towel again. "Old man, a book can have Chicago in it, and not be about Chicago. It can have a tennis player in it without being about a tennis player."
> I didn't get it. I probably looked it, for he went on, "Take this book here, old man—" and he held up one of the books he had swiped from some library. Along with the numbers I could see Hemingway's name on the spine. "There's a prizefighter in it, old man, but it's not about a prizefighter."
> "Is it about the sun rising?" I said. I knew that was part of the title.
> "Goddam if I know what it's about," he said . . .

I   The Southpaw

Nevertheless, even if only under the heading of verisimilitude, the novels are also about baseball. At any rate, the baseball parts of the setting are centrally and lovingly handled:

> In the years since the publication of *The Southpaw* the question I am most commonly asked is, "How did you ever know so much about baseball?" Alas, I confess it was amateur love. The only professional players

I met were a few Denver Bears one night. Since then, mainly on magazine assignment, I have met some of the "real" people of the game, though confronting them, and spying on their secret meetings, or even listening for the meaning hidden beyond the word, has told me very little I hadn't already known or guessed. The man of fiction, Henry James tells us, takes an ell when he's handed an inch. I knew, not so much by going and looking as by sitting and analogizing, and by reading between the lines of the gross newspaper fact."[1]

While the second and third books of the trilogy might be too complicated for someone whose primary interest was baseball rather than literature, since one deals with attitudes toward death and the other with attitudes toward reality, I suspect that the first (and best) of the novels could be read with pleasure by ordinary fans. It chronicles Henry Wiggen's life from the time he is playing baseball for his high school down to the time he is voted most valuable player in the National League; and the climactic moments of the novel, accordingly, are his first seeing a major-league ballgame, his being discovered by a scout and offered a contract, his first spring tryouts for the majors in Florida, his coming to the majors and pitching his first game, and so on, down to winning the World Series. Moreover, these climaxes are not treated satirically or symbolically but quite straightforwardly, as the intended climaxes of the novel. The account of the way it feels to play the game seems utterly convincing, even instructive.

For these reasons I suspect an unsophisticated person interested in baseball might enjoy reading the book, missing a great deal, no doubt, but not missing everything. The book is about the course of a man's life, and since the man happens to be a baseball player, we can only get the full feeling of it by having the baseball given to us truly and fully. This is why the sophisticated reader who would not walk across a room to see a baseball game can also read the book with enjoyment. Man—whatever he does—is still the most interesting animal around, and when his life is presented with truth, the result is willy-nilly philosophy, willy-nilly allegory, any man once more becoming Everyman.

Harris speaks of the time he began working on *The Southpaw*, when he was a graduate student at the University of Denver in 1951. "My friends, who were nervous beginners and ridden with caution, were often most traditional. Baseball was for boys, they said, not for literature, but I wrote my book anyhow, out of the faith that if I was moved and amused by what I was writing somebody else was bound to be, betting on my humanity that way" (Introduction).

I want to identify here the special kind of symbolism Harris employs. Malamud in *The Natural* uses a baseball player striving for perfection to represent a knight questing for the Holy Grail. The Fisher King and other mythological characters are thinly disguised under baseball jerseys. Robert Coover in the *Universal Baseball Association* has a baseball league owner who represents Jehovah (J. Henry Waugh) with his teams symbolizing the world. These are novels to delight the sophisticated reader, but our unlettered baseball buff who enjoyed *The Southpaw* would drop them pretty quickly. I am not disparaging either type of novel, since I enjoy both, but I am trying to place the special qualities of Harris's. His symbolism is akin to Frost's, which is to say closer to synecdoche than symbol. Frost uses a fork in the road to symbolize A Fork in the Road. Harris uses a man's life to symbolize A Man's Life. The terms do not change—baseball player to knight—rather, they extend—any man to Everyman.

II *The Language*

"The baseball books," Harris has said, "are written out of a rebellion against formal language."[2] This is a bit of an overstatement, for (as he once admitted to me), he was also following an established literary tradition which dates at least to Huck Finn, of the naïve and semiliterate narrator telling his story in his own language. This language (I am speaking of the three novels together in this section) can be a source of comedy in its own right in its solecisms and nonsequiturs, as when a character is trying to think of someone's name and Henry says, "Probably some morning when you wake up his name will be right there on your tongue." Or, speaking of another player's home town, "he lives in Mill on the road to Climax, which got its name on account of an old mill there that long ago broke down.[3] At its best, Henry may, as Harris puts it, "here and there, be able to say something that punctures our thinking quite effectively by his own simplicity."[4] I have mentioned, for example, his speaking of "the war against Korea."

For the most part, the language is merely appropriate, the language Harris heard when he was in the army, or heard spoken in poor neighborhoods he lived in.[5] *Could have* is regularly *could of; than* is always *then; lie, lay;* and so on. Past participles are consistently garbled, *brought* becoming *brung, swung* becoming *swang. One* is written *1*. This means that the reader accustoms himself to this sublanguage so that, while it never loses its appropriateness, and while it can occasionally be a source of humor or insight, it is for the most part unobtrusive. Most important, at moments of high emotion, it proves itself a perfectly adequate medium of expression.

Harris is genuinely revolutionary in at least one respect, and perhaps ill-advisedly so. Early on in *The Southpaw*, when he is quoting someone else's speech, Henry warns us,

> I don't know if those was his exact words. When I put down words that I say somebody said they needn't be the exact words, just what you might call the meaning. You must keep that in mind as you plow on through this book. Many a time in the Mammoth clubhouse the writers will say to the skipper, "Dutch, what do you think about so-and-so or this and that?" and Dutch will say, "I think that so-and-so or this and that is a load of crap." The next day I will look, and they have wrote, "Mammoth manager Dutch Schnell expressed the opinion that so-and-so or this and that will probably never come to pass" and a lot more fancy words which I guess what they amount to is the same load of crap Dutch was referring to in the first place (pp. 22 - 23).

Of course what Henry does is just the opposite. As a sort of reverse Thucydides,[6] he reduces the presumably more elegant speech of the better educated among the characters to his own argot. This is, after all, consistent with the book's premise that it is being written by Henry, who perhaps can write down, but not up. It is a more radical consistency than we usually ask for in such a book, however. Occasionally there is a nice humor in hearing, for instance, his wife's uncle, an educated and literate professional astronomer, say, "I brung you a little something" (p. 74), or the wealthy glittering society lady, Patricia Moors, say, "Leave us look at a few pictures" (p. 101). But in general we are not aware that this is the intention, and critics are prone to object that "his characters all talk alike,"[7] which of course is true, and perhaps a little richness of dialogue has been sacrificed to methodological consistency.

At its worst, the language can be repetitious, predictable, "mannered"—at times, just a bit tiresome, a box Harris cannot get out of. He certainly began to worry about it more and more himself. In speaking, long afterwards, of *Bang the Drum Slowly*, the second book of the trilogy, he told the cautionary tale of Ring Lardner (who, with Twain, was another obvious influence on his writing): "To use the phrase that Edmund Wilson used in connection with Ring Lardner, 'you must now tell us what you know.' In the end Lardner couldn't tell us because he didn't have the language for it; besides, he had made his reputation with the colloquial, the oral, the slang tradition, and he couldn't break from it. People didn't want him to talk any better; they wanted him to talk in the same language."[8]

Not that Henry is static, not that Henry is not learning and growing himself, as he matures from book to book. "At the mature pace," Harris tells us, projecting into the future of his character, "he says it better now, less awkward, less profane, not now in the vulgar tongue, tighter now, with absolute economy and fierce compression. Not with less passion, but in fewer words" (Introduction). But here perhaps as so often he is mixing Henry's career with his own, for after the first two books—and a third which may not have been written had it not been specially commissioned—he went to more literate protagonists or spoke in his own voice. "For what I know now, I simply need a fuller English, and when one feels this necessity, it would be a kind of self-violation not to go through with it."[9]

III The Characters

The Southpaw is a novel particularly rich in characters: Henry and his family and friends, all the ballplayers, trainers, managers, owners, sportswriters, even members of opposing teams. The miracle is how well-realized, how completely individual and convincing each character is. The least character becomes a living presence, and when he comes up to play his part, to pinch-hit, or to face Wiggen's pitching at a crucial moment, we already know him, know what is at stake for him, how he is likely to act or react. The round, the convincing, the "felt" character: this, it seems to me, novel after novel, is Harris's great strength.

In this novel even the major characters are numerous. They seem to arrange themselves into three groups: (1) those who have given up their own lives to the "organization"—in this case, to the vast Moors empire, the industrialist owners of the baseball team; (2) those who, on the contrary, care in life only for themselves; and (3) those who, rejecting the "organization," similarly reject pure selfishness, and choose instead to live in a small community of chosen individuals. Henry—since this is a coming-of-age novel—is cast adrift into this tripartite world, observing and provisionally joining one group and then the other, before at last finding himself. The character who most grotesquely epitomizes the first category is the team secretary, Bradley Lord:

Bradley is a frog. You know how a frog does. When he is sitting on the ground you give him a little touch on the behind and up he leaps and starts to run. If Mr. Moors or Patricia Moors is to say a word up he jumps and begins to do what was said. Naturally they don't go over and touch him on the behind, but it adds up to the same thing. One time in the Mammoth clubhouse I was sitting with Red when in come Bradley Lord, and he walked past, and Red said to him, "you are a frog. Did you ever think to yourself what a frog you were?" Bradley Lord said he never considered himself as a frog. "Yet at least," said Red, "a frog will sometime not jump when he is touched on the behind, for at least sometime a frog has got the sense to lay down and die and not be a frog no longer" (pp. 101 - 102).

Patricia Moors, daughter of old Mr. Moors, to whom the club has been given as a sort of personal plaything, has—in a more complex way—similarly given herself up to the organization. Beautiful, young and rich, shrewd, ambitious, she has nonetheless left herself with nothing. At one point we see her spending the night in a motel with one of the team's least attractive players, "Ugly" Jones, in order to get him to settle for a contract of $2,000 less per year. Once, candidly envying Henry, she speaks bitterly of her impersonal role:

"A ball player need only do his job," she said. "He need never entertain the owner of a paper so as to get a decent treatment in the press. It does not matter what the press says. A home run is a home run and no 2 ways about it. . . ."
"Yet there must be people to keep the organization running on all fours," I said.
"That is the part that is closed from sight," said she. "That is the part that any cluck can do. There is 5,000 people in this park this minute that can step in and do what I do. But it is mine because I was born to it. My name is Patricia Moors. What gives me the chills is suppose my name was Betty Brown" (p. 263).

We often see the cost to her of this sacrifice of self, see her falling down drunk at her own opulent parties, throwing up into her own swimming pool. "All that good liquor gone down the drain to nowheres, just like me. Did you follow me, Wiggen?" (161).

Unlike Bradley Lord, the potential was there for something better: "She is one of these women caught halfway between keeping house for some cluck and really *doing* something in life" (p. 264).

Yet the opposite tack, of doing everything strictly for the self, does not seem any more satisfactory. This position is best exemplified by "Sad Sam" Yale, long the star left-handed pitcher, now just a bit over the hill as Henry joins the team. He had been Henry's boyhood idol, so the first view Henry has of him at spring training, fat and balding, running around the field in a rubber suit to get back to his weight, is a bit of a shock. "I am an old man rushed in my grave by women and liquor," Sam tells him (p. 86).

But mortality itself is not the issue, since all men share this. Sad Sam had the ability, and single-mindedly pushed himself to the top. He is still so fine that when he pitches, Henry (who is not otherwise modest) drops everything he is doing to watch him and learn from him. But in puzzling ways everything has gone sour for Sam:

"Those that aim high when they get there finds out that they should of went somewheres else. You think you want money and then you get it and you piss it away because it ain't what you really wanted in the first place. You think you want your name in the headline, but you get it there and that ain't what you want neither. You think you want this woman or that woman, and then you get the money and the headlines and the woman besides. Then you find out you do not want the woman no more and probably never wanted her in the first place."

"That is right," said I.

"How would you know?" he said. "It will take you 15 years to find out. You get so you do not care. It is all like a ball game with nobody watching and nobody keeping score and nobody behind you. You pitch hard and nobody really cares. Nobody really gives a f———— what happens to anybody else." He looked very sad. . . .

"*Sad* Sam Yale," I said.

"I ain't sad," he said. "I just do not care. I just play for the money I do not need and fornicate for the kicks I never get. . . . If I was to write a book they would never print it. It would be 5 words long. It would say, Do Not F———— With Me. I would send it to every church and every schoolhouse and tell them to hang it up over their door. It will not get you anywheres in life. But it is the best you can ask for *out* of life. The best you can hope is that everybody else will just leave you alone" (pp. 238 - 39).

Dutch Schnell, the team manager, almost embodies both poles. Like Sad Sam he has achieved personal greatness, and he has done it by caring for nobody, only single-mindedly pursuing success. And yet in his efforts to win at any cost, he has finally given up his personality to identify almost completely with the game:

Everybody always asks me, "What kind of man is Dutch Schnell?" I never know exactly what to say. I think he is a great manager, and the statistics back me up in this. His first and only aim in life is winning ball games, and more often he wins them then not, sometimes doing it with worse material then the next club has got. He brings out the best in a fellow if the fellow is his type of ballplayer. . . . There is nothing Dutch will not do for the sake of the ball game. If he thinks it will help win a ball game by eating you out he will eat you out. If sugar and honey will do the trick out comes the sugar and honey bottle. If it is money you need he will give you money. And if he has no further need for you he will sell you or trade you or simply cut you loose and forget you (p. 330).

Ultimately, though, for all his canniness, his toughness, his dedication, he has become a piece of machinery operating efficiently for the Moors empire. When he falters, he too will be cast aside.

He is most obviously to be contrasted with jovial Mike Mulrooney, manager of the Queen City Cowboys, the AA team where Henry had his first two years of seasoning in the pros. Mike, who is as universally loved as Dutch is hated, puts his boys first, getting the most out of them, bringing them to their full potential. He is a great teacher, a simple, religious, good-hearted man, and his teams do well enough. But the novel does not sentimentalize. Compared to Dutch, he is minor league. Dutch could not have gotten where he is any other way. The book does not suggest that the means could have been different; it questions whether the ends justify them.

There is no doubt who the good characters are in the book, for they all share the same qualities. There is nothing puling or mawkish about them. They tend to be crusty nonconformists. They too strive to win, to succeed—but only to the point that winning does not interfere with their personal pride, their sense of their own integrity. They are haters of sham, lovers of honesty. Their hearts are not closed to others, but their real care is only for those who meet their high standards. Politically they are pacifists, socially they are—when need be—rebels. Their measures of success are not money and headlines. They are as uncompromising as the other characters but their loyalty is neither to themselves purely, nor to some abstract organization, but rather to some high and best notion of their humanity.

Among these characters there is Henry's "pop." He was in his own time a promising young southpaw pitcher who seemed to be on his way to fame in the big leagues. But "Pop has a mind of his own" (p. 15). He was just starting out in minor-league ball, having a very good season, almost ready to be sent up to the majors. "The exact story on what happened after the second year is still not clear in my mind and probably never will be. . . . All I know is that Pop simply up and quit after the second summer at Cedar Rapids. He done this in despite of the fact that his wife that he married the previous winter was expecting a baby" (p. 16). We are made to feel he quit on some personal principle, that despite the obvious tremendous cost to himself and his family, when the time came, he chose for his own integrity. He returned to his hometown in Perkinsville to play semi-pro ball two nights a week, and support himself the rest of the time driving the school bus or tending the grounds of the observatory next door to him. Mainly he painstakingly taught Henry all he knew and carefully brought him along to his first professional contract.

Aaron, the thoughtful and learned man who manages the observatory next door, also has a mind of his own:

The government wanted to use the Observatory during the war, but Aaron turned them down. Aaron rules the whole works under orders from his group of scientists and it can be used only to look at the stars and moon and such. . . . I was very young when the argument with the Government took place, but I remember there was a good deal of discussion in the papers, not only in Perkinsville but everywhere, Aaron holding fast and finally winning out, and you have got to admire him for that. He is over 80 years old. . . . If you ever stop at the Observatory he will come right up to you, squinting and looking at you, and tell you his name and pop right out with questions and answers, what do you think of this and that and your politics" (p. 14).

Red Traphagen, the crusty intellectual catcher for the Mammoths, is the only one who knows Spanish and so can communicate with the Cuban player on the team. "Red learned it at Harvard plus which he also spent some time in Spain in the war there" (p. 30). "The temptestuous redhead," a sportswriter writes, is "popular with the fans again after his eccentric war-time behavior" (p. 188) but still refuses to stand for the National Anthem before games, cynically grumbling, "land of the free and home of the brave. There ain't a 1 of them free and there ain't 200 of them brave. 25,-000 sheep" (p. 204). And last there is Holly, Aaron's niece, bright and pretty and gentle but fiercely prideful in her own way. "When she was a little kid she used to live partly in Baltimore with her own folks and partly with Aaron, there being a running family squabble between her mother and her father for many years. When she was 18 she come and lived with Aaron for good, hating and detesting her own folks and giving them no end of trouble until they turned her loose" (p. 25). Later, we hear, "she become permanent at Aaron's about that time, having went for awhile to college at New Rochelle but in 6 months was in hot water 6 times and finally pooped out and as far as I know was never missed" (p. 39). Long before Henry has any interest in girls she picks him out to be her man, and when he tells her of his first bumbling and unconsummated amorous encounter with Thedabara Brown, which has left him with "most unusual pains in and around [his] groin" (p. 44), Holly quickly takes him into her own bed, to make sure her own claim is staked. But, nevertheless, when he gets into the big leagues and, flushed with self-importance at being on his way to enormous success, he proposes to her at every chance she holds him off, waiting to find out if Henry the Navigator, as she calls him, will come through his sea of temptation still worthy of his best self, still with the pride and integrity that she demands of him.

These characters are all settled in their positions. It is only Henry who is up for grabs. He is brash, cocky, full of himself and his undeniable talents, green, worshiping Sad Sam, physically attracted to Patricia Moors, and forgetful of Pop and Aaron and Holly when they are not right beside him to give him their sound advice. But he has a saving hard core of decency—it is what they had all seen in him to begin with—with their same hatred of sham, though with his immaturity it takes him longer to recognize it for what it is. He is innately pacifistic, with a medical deferment from military service since even the sight of violence causes his bowels to loosen.

Old Aaron, seeing him off when he leaves to play professional ball, realizes the temptations ahead for him and tries, knowing it is useless, to give him some guidance:

"We cannot pass along our knowledge. Young people must learn for themself. I am just hoping, Henry, that no matter if you fail or succeed in what you are about to try that you will keep your ways. You have always looked at things in a good way, finding the good things good and the boring things a bore. It would do no good for me to tell you that the bright world of glitter and glamor that you are heading towards is nothing but Graduation Night at Perkinsville High plus Tom Swallow's Texaco Station. It is all a lot of hardware tinsel to cover the fact of the bore."

"It is 25 of," I said. "The train is at 6" (p. 73).

IV *Henry Wiggen as Tom Jones*

Henry is an American Tom Jones, but with talent to recommend him instead of blood. His sublunary reward is to realize the American dream of becoming a baseball hero, winning over twenty games in his first season in the majors, playing in the All-Star Game and the World Series, and being voted Most Valuable Player. Tom Jones in the end realizes the eighteenth-century version of this dream, becoming a gentleman, marrying a beautiful heiress with a swinging fortune and vast estate. But in each case the earthly success is secondary to the spiritual one of achieving the wisdom to give the success its proper valuation. Tom, without always knowing it, and sometimes going dangerously astray, is seeking his Sophia ("wisdom") as Henry is seeking his Holly, whose character if not her name has the same signification. They are improvident and impulsive young men, and the outcome of their quests is often very much in doubt.

Henry, in a more realistic novel, is more consistent as a character than Tom. His speech does not change from time to time so that he can become a spokesman for his author; his personality does not alter at various points for the sake of underlining some thematic statement. More consistent, he is less manic, more restrained. He is never quite so spontaneously good-natured as Tom, never modest or self-effacing ("Pop says you got to believe in yourself"—p. 17). On the other hand, he is never quite so unconventional as Tom either, as in the really nasty scenes where Tom prostitutes himself to Lady Bellaston. Henry's sins, with one exception, are of intention rather than commission. Nevertheless, in their trampings from place to place, in the contrasts between home in the small town and the bright lights of the city, in the friends, the advisers, the tempters, the promise and the danger, the books are parallel.

The night before Henry leaves for his first season in the majors, Holly "give me the best advice anyone ever give me concerning baseball and how to play it. She said, 'Henry, you must play ball like it does not matter, for it really does not matter. Nothing really matters. Play ball, do your best, have fun, but do not put the game nor the cash before your own personal pride,' and I said I would" (p. 135). The problem is, he will be gone from her good advice all season, and she is not really sure of him. In the heat of all his emotions of leaving her and starting out in his career, he proposes to her, and she says no. "But we will see what Old Father Time brings forth" (p. 135).

Time indeed provides the important rhythm of this book, time for the athlete running faster than for the rest of us. In the clubhouse "life is short, dismissal imminent, the rivalries brutal, and we are all anxiety" (Introduction). As a boy he goes to see his first major-league game, to watch Sad Sam Yale pitch, his idol, the man who, in another few years, he will replace. He and his father look at Sam's picture in the paper. "Pop said he looked old. He was then just turned 30" (p. 49).

As a regular feature of the novel, each time Henry advances a rung on the ladder, it is at the expense of someone else. When young Henry first shows his stuff to the manager of the semipro team his father pitches for, the manager "said he would sign me on as batting practice pitcher and fire this other kid and maybe later I would work in in relief and maybe after that as a starter" (p. 42). In fact he gets his first break when his father, the regular pitcher, has a bad day and falters. Henry comes in for him, and in an eerily significant moment "I seen Pop on the bench and it seemed like he was somewheres where he ought not to been, and I looked for myself and could not find myself though I ought to been sitting on the bench and was not" (p. 60).

He alternates starts with his father after that, the team's other pitcher, Slim Doran, being fired to make room for him. When he works his way up to the major leagues "Bub Castetter . . . was cut loose just this past year to make room for me. Somebody is always getting the ax for my sake—the batting-practice kid at Perkinsville, then Slim Doran, then a fellow name of Duckworth at Queen City, and finally Bud in May of 52. I suppose that right now there is somewheres a kid in short pants that will someday crowd me out" (p. 93).

Within this abbreviated time span Henry has a lot of growing up to do. It is a question of learning what is valuable. At first he values himself chiefly as a ballplayer, but in chilling moments he realizes that as a ballplayer he is merely a cog in the Moors machinery. His first insight comes in the year in which, as a green kid, he is signed by a scout to his first contract. He naïvely wanders into the Main Moors office in New York to introduce himself. No one in the office, naturally, has any idea who he is, and when, baffled, he asks them why they seem to be laughing at him, " 'The reason I am laughing,' said the man, 'is this,' and he went over to the wall where there was 3 green cabinets, and he begun to slide some drawers out as far as they would go, and he run his hand up and down the papers in the drawer. 'Records,' he said. 'Every 1 of these papers is a record on some kid that thinks he is another Joe DiMaggio. . . . They are just names. Your name is somewhere amongst them. . . . You are but another name!' " p. 77).

Shaken, he vows to himself that he will become something more. But he still speaks in the wrong terms. He vows that one day nine out of ten people on the street will know his name, and indeed he ultimately wins such recognition, but he has still not shown Holly who *he* is, and she still refuses him.

As Aaron writes to him, in a letter of affectionate advice, "Only sorely troubled human beings need success in the accepted sense; the wise are content to turn their back upon it and to own, if not the Moors 'empire,' the love and respect of a few neighbors of moderate means, little 'success' and no visible ambition" (p. 279).

Unfortunately, Henry fails his first important test. The Mammoths have been leading the league all season, but toward the end they go into a slump. Tempers shorten, the men fight among themselves, filled with insecurity as rumors mount that this one or that may be traded off (a frightening reminder that to the Moors empire they have no human value, but are only commodities). Under the continuing tension Henry develops a psychosomatic back complaint. In a crucial game this interferes with his full motion, and his curves stop breaking. He is facing Tubs Blodgett, an amiable and well-liked player on the opposing team. It is a tight moment in the game, and in desperation Henry wipes the sweat off his forehead with his hand and, his fingers still wet, pitches a curve:

That is what you call a spitter. It is outlawed from baseball. A player can pull a suspension for a year if he throws it, for you can kill a man with a spitter if you hit him right. You do not have it under full control. All this I knowed, and I did not care. I did not wish to kill Tubs Blodgett, but my curve was not breaking on account of my back, and I throwed quick before I had time to think about consequences, and the curve broke big and sharp,

for my fingers was slimy and wet, and Tubs swang and missed, striking out
and ending the inning. Red whipped it down towards third, like he was
making the play on Chickering coming down from second, and George
never even reached for the throw but left it roll to the outfield, for the roll-
ing dried it off (p. 298).

It was obvious to everyone what he had done, but it could not be
proved, and so he got away with it. "Dutch . . . said I must not do
it again, and he laughed" (p. 229), but we hear later that Pop,
watching the game on television, wept when he saw it. Henry has
forgotten Holly's advice; he has put the game and the cash before
his personal pride. When he proposes to her again, she again
refuses. He tells her how much money he is making.

"Is that how you have learned to measure things?" said she. "Do you
now measure a man by the size of his pay?"
"I measure people like everybody else measures them," [he says defensively, and wonders if she would prefer him to pump gas somewhere].
"It is not a matter of me marrying either you or a gas pumper. It is a
matter of marrying a man . . . but you are losing your manhood faster
than hell . . . and becoming simply an island in the empire of Moors"
(pp. 305 - 306).

But though he has "begun to understand . . . that time was running out with her and me" (p. 304) he continues—when she is
away—to be sexually attracted to Patricia Moors, beautiful, jingling
with rich jewelry, symbol of everything spuriously glamorous in his
dreams of success.
Soon, all the dreams are realized. He—or at least his name—is
known to the man on the street. He has won his twenty-odd games,
pitched in the All-Star Game, and finally won the pennant. To his
amazement, all he feels is disillusionment and disgust. At the huge
victory party he sees players who had been bitter enemies all season
"murmuring sweet little things in 1 another's ears"; he sees the
team's one black player "buttering up" Swanee Wilks, the outspoken racist. Lester T. Moors, owner of the team, praises Henry,
though he might have sold him off earlier in the season.
"Oh, winning heals many a wound in the flesh! And I could not
help thinking, 'What if we lost? What if 6 games between April and
September had went the other way? What then? Would Perry and
Swanee be drinking together? Would Red and Sam Yale? . . . And
suppose I only won 13 games instead of 26? Would I then be the little golden apple in the eye of Lester T. Moors, Jr.?" (p. 335).

These are friends in victory only, and the friendship is for what they have done, not for what they are. But Holly had asked him before: Who would like him when the chips were down? He hears Patricia Moors calling for him, but instead he rushes from the party, hurries home to Holly.

"You dream and you dream and you dream, and then when the dream comes true it falls flat on its face."

"Not *my* dream," said she. "According to my dream this was to be a year of great victory for you, and I believe it was."

"The statistics back you up in that," said I.

"Oh no," said she, "they show nothing of the sort. They show only games won and games lost and your E.R.A. and such as that. What they do not show is that you growed to manhood over the summer. You will throw no more spitballs for the sake of something so stupid as a ball game. You will worship the feet of no more gods name of Sad Sam Yale nor ever be a true follower of Dutch Schnell. . . . You will never be an island in the empire of Moors, Henry, and that is the great victory that hardly anybody wins any more."

"I believe it is at that," said I. "I never thought about it much. Yet I thought about it a little bit at that, noticing how even the boys theirselves buckled and lost their courage when the heat was on."

"The boys are no different then anybody else," she said. "The boys are the world, and they are ruled by their belly and their fear. You have learned to do different, and I hope you will always go on following your head and your heart and the things that they tell you about men and money and what happens to courage when the heat is on."

"I will try," said I (p. 348).

V Henry as "Author"

Henry is not quite Everyman. There is a characteristic indirection: Henry is Everyman as Artist, and his identity as writer of the baseball novels begins to merge with Harris's as writer of baseball novels. He is, after all, one of Harris's "disguises."

This can be seen in a number of different ways. First there is Henry's self-consciousness over the writing of his book. His life is only the material of the book. With Holly's and Aaron's and Red's advice, and his own growing tact, he begins to shape these materials. In the first chapter he briefly introduces himself and his family and then concludes, "That's it. Those are the folks and also the end of the chapter. Holly says try to write up 1 thing only in every chapter and don't be wandering all over the lot, and then, when the subject is covered, break it off and begin another" (p. 18).

Following chapter 11 in the book is Chapter 11 - A, in which he tells about the long debate he had with his friends before finally throwing out Chapter 12 altogether. He thought it was his best chapter, telling in detail all the games he played his two years in the minor leagues, describing each city they visited, giving capsule biographies of different characters. But Aaron tells him "that is too much space to give to things of such little importance" (107).

"That is a lot of rubbage," said I. "If you have got the sense to think back on chapter 11 you will remember that it run 9 pages front to back between the time Sid Goldman hit the home run, about 3 o'clock, until midnight. That is 9 pages covering 9 hours, while this is 9 pages covering 3 *weeks*. . . ."
"But the things that happened in number 11," said he, "was important. . . . I actually think that the whole exhibition trip could be knocked off in 1 page" (p. 107).

It is a good classical principle of composition that is being outlined, the same that is seen in one of Fielding's digressions on aesthetics in *Tom Jones* (Bk. II, Chap. 1).
In the same chapter Henry had written a long description of his minor-league manager "part of it copied out of a book called 'Forty-One Diamond Immortals' " (p. 107). Holly takes him to task:

"About 1 dozen times you said Mike Mulrooney is 1 of the grandest men that ever lived. That is not saying anything."
"The hell it ain't," said I, "for if you knowed Mike you would say the same."
"I do not say that Mike is not all you say," said she, "but you must tell us why."
"Because he *is*," said I. "Because he does not wish to run the whole show but just live an easy going life and not worry you ragged about setting the whole world on fire. Because if you make a mistake he will not eat you out in front of all the rest nor give you the icy glare every time he runs into you in the hotel. He will stand by you and not go about talking behind your back. He will treat you all the same, no matter if you are on the way up or the way down, for he takes the attitude that if you are not the greatest ballplayer in the world still and all you are a human being. . . ."
"Excellent. . . . You have told us more about Mr. Mulrooney right there than you done in the 9 pages of Chapter 12 concerned with him" (p. 108).

Show, don't tell, in other words—a major aesthetic to Harris.

In somewhat more indirect ways Harris draws many parallels between the life of a ballplayer and the life of an artist—both, of course, being performers for the public.

Henry is watching boys playing ball in a sandlot (cp. Harris watching the students in his creative-writing classes): "You always think when you see them that maybe right there before your eyes is some immortal of tomorrow, for 1 of the beautiful things about the game is that the immortals rise up from nowhere" (p. 80).

There is the reiteration of a common notion of Harris's (almost, himself, a compulsive writer): "A ballplayer has got to play ball like a singer has got to sing and an artist has got to draw pictures and a mountain climber has got to have a mountain to climb or else go crazy" (139).

There are obvious parallels between the sportswriters and the hack review writers: "They are like the plague. There is not 1 of them that has got the guts and gumption to get out there and play ball theirselves, yet they know just exactly how the game should be played. They will get the fatigue from climbing 6 steps, yet they know how Perry Simpson should steal a base. They will get a cramp in their arm from writing a few words down on paper yet if a ballplayer pitches 7 innings and poops out they are as libel as not to decide he is a quitter. . . . Yet ballplayers read the papers day and night" (p. 125).

Henry's attitude toward most of the fans is just that of a frustrated serious writer: "That is the way it always is. The fans will clap and cheer at something that anybody knows is bad baseball. Then on a good play, something that is really hard to pull off, they will sit there like their arm was paralyzed and their jaw broke" (156).

In some of Harris's own statements about Henry, the closeness of their identification with one another becomes evident. "Henry's left arm is his fortune, but his ear is his soul. He listens not to what people say but to what they mean. His report upon what he hears is frank, but he is armed against reprisal: his enemies, since they are invariably malicious (which is to say, stupid), have not the ears to know they have been condemned. If the reader is himself without ears (which is to say, untrained to read) he will think Henry untrained to write. He will think Henry is nothing but a baseball player,"[10] just as some of Harris's readers think he writes novels which are about nothing but baseball.

And finally, speculating on Henry's future, Harris writes:

Probably he will become a manager of men, and succeed, for baseball taught him everything, as an art teaches. He took ells for inches by guess and by hunch. His pace is mature now . . . he says it better now, less awkward. . . . Not with less passion but in fewer words. All the things he hated then he hates still—exploitation and false report. . . . What Henry did best was to turn his hatred to style and story, and so shine good. He knew to keep from imitating hate. Above all, he wrote his own book in his own voice, suffering consequences along with rewards" (Introduction).

VI   Bang the Drum Slowly

As this novel begins, Henry has been in the majors for four years. A certain amount of reality, and the beginnings of wisdom, have been forced upon him. In the accelerated time of the professional athlete, he is already an old hand. In his first year up he had been the youngest player on the team. Now there are nine men younger than he. A number of older players have gone. Since the writing of *The Southpaw* (he is now nicknamed "Author" by his teammates) he has had two poor seasons: "In the summer of 52 I was the toast of New York, but 2 years later I couldn't of got a traffic ticket squashed (p. 6).[11] Not that he has learned anything approaching modesty: "All that was wrong with me was the team wasn't hitting" (p. 17). Also, he has played badly because of money worries. He got into a Joe Louis - like situation with a huge tax arrears which he could not pay off because, when he earned more money to pay it off, the new earnings only further increased his tax burden. His case was finally settled in court, but now he has taken a hard line on money. "I used to pee away money like wine, until I got wise to myself" (p. 6). He is playing winter ball in Cuba and Mexico and Japan, he is on the banquet circuit, and he is industriously selling Arcturus insurance to his fellow ballplayers. He has turned his income tax over to Holly, and the two of them are looking at everything in terms of possible tax deductions, even to the child with which Holly is three months pregnant. As Henry leaves the house: "Take care of 600 Dollars,' I said, which was what we kept calling him before she was born" (p. 6).

The title, *Bang the Drum Slowly,* is a mangled line out of the "Streets of Laredo," a song about a cowboy dying young. In this novel Henry, as a further step in his maturity, will learn about that which makes the game, money, and almost everything else a secondary matter.

His roommate, Bruce Pearson, third-string catcher on the team, phones him during the winter from his hospital bed in Rochester, Minnesota, telling Henry he must come out and see him. After flying to Minnesota, Henry becomes enraged to see Bruce looking fit and healthy until he learns Bruce is, as Bruce puts it, "doomeded." He has Hodgkin's disease, and though appearing perfectly healthy, he could die at any time from six weeks to fifteen years. Henry starts to phone Dutch, then thinks twice about it, because Bruce wants to play. If Dutch knew, he would put the team's interests first and immediately fire Bruce. Henry promises secrecy, telling only Holly, but that means that all season long he must carry by himself the burden of his knowledge.

His perspective immediately changes. "You would be surprised if you listen to the number of times a day people tell you something will last a lifetime or tell you something killed them, or tell you they are dead. 'I was simply dead,' they say, 'He killed me,' 'I am dying,' which I never noticed before but now begun to notice more and more" (p. 14).

The problem is that Bruce is not a very good catcher. Red Traphagen, the brilliant first-string catcher, has quit to become a college teacher. The other catchers are problematical for one reason or another: "Goose" is old and dissipated, no more legs, no arm; Johah Brooks is a fine catcher but cannot hit; Bruce is a natural athlete but not very bright, has no "science," misses his signs, cannot remember what any of the batters hit; and so on. According to Dutch, "He was $1,000,000 worth of promise worth 2¢ on delivery" (p. 195). Dutch badly needs a first-rate catcher, and is contemplating bringing up a promising but scatterbrained motorcycle-riding young man named Piney Woods. If he does, Bruce would be released. Henry, who has been holding out on his contract for the year, makes a desperate move. "Sir," he tells Mr. Moor, "there is one clause yet to go in my contract. . . . There must be a clause . . . saying that me and Bruce Pearson will stay with the club together, or else go together. Whatever happens to one must happen to the other, traded or sold or whatever. We must be tied in a package on any deal under the sun" (p. 67).

Dutch's response is natural: "This is telling me who I must keep and who not. . . . Talking money is one thing. But talking business is another, and I will as soon trade the whole club for a tin

of beans as leave anybody tell me who stays and who gets cut loose"
(p. 67). But when Henry convinces him he is in dead earnest, Dutch
gives in. "I will agree to this clause. I never done such a thing
before and would not do it now except there is a look in your eye
that tells me that I must" (p. 71). But the unusual clause, and
rumors of mysterious meetings between Henry and Bruce during
the winter, have made Dutch vow to get to the bottom of things. He
begins quizzing Bruce and Henry, and hires a private detective to
snoop around. At the same time the secret is leaking to more and
more people, making it a matter of time before it gets back to
Dutch.

VII *Henry's Extra Weight*

At this point I would like to begin pointing out how effective the
organization of the novel is. The inevitable action around which all
three baseball novels are built is the season itself. But it is in the
present novel that it is most intricately woven into the theme.[12] At
the beginning of the season, on paper, the Mammoths are far and
away the best team: they have the best pitching, the best outfield,
the best double-play combination, the best left- and right-hand hitting, with only the weakness in catching. These statistics are borne
out later when a full seven members of the team are selected for the
All-Star Game, more than from any other team.

As the season progresses, however, it becomes apparent that
something is wrong. "Dutch kept tinkering. . . . He kept juggling
the order, and when that didn't work he kept juggling the
bench . . . seeing what I seen and what the boys would of also
seen if they cut out the horseshit long enough. . . . It was not pulling like a club. It was 2 ½ and 3 and 3 ½ on top all through the
west, but it should of been 4 ½ or 5 by now. . . . The club was not
a club" (pp. 117 - 20).

Henry is pitching very well, and one or two players are hitting
well, "but you cannot go all the way on a few bats or a few arms"
(p. 120). Henry has come into the season eight or nine pounds
above his playing weight, but this does not bother him, as the
weight seems to make him fast and accurate, and beneath the surface we realize that that other weight he is carrying, the knowledge
that his teammate is dying before his eyes, is also making him play
better. The other players do not see, as he does, the appalling
shortness of life, do not value it properly, are wasting their time

bickering and fighting with each other. Bruce with his slow wits is the particular victim of their cruel ragging, and the players, noticing the sudden closeness between Henry and Bruce, have taken to calling them Romeo and Juliet.

Bruce's own heightened sense of the value of life is making him play better as well. Coming out of the dream he has always played in, he begins to keep a book on opposing pitchers. One pitcher the teams finds particularly difficult to hit, Bruce notices, always throws him a curve ball once he has gotten two strikes on him. Bruce, standing at the plate with two strikes on him, waits for the curve and leans in and powders it, saving the game. He begins paying attention, listening to the tips his teammates give him, and as Dutch begins playing him more and more, he begins hitting consistently and even catching more intelligently.

Everything delights him. " 'I like sweating,' said Bruce. 'I like hitting. Sometimes I even like popping out, looking up there and seeing how high you drove it. . . . I love stinking . . . and coming in and ripping off your clothes and getting under the shower and thinking about eating' " (p. 188).

This becomes a pattern. One player is ragging Bruce particularly fiercely, and Henry, to stop him, finally breaks down and tells him Bruce is dying. The player swears secrecy, becomes friendly with Henry and Bruce, begins treating his own wife better, quits running around, and settles down and begins to play serious ball. One by one the players learn, and one by one they come up to Bruce with spontaneous acts of friendship. The ragging, the backbiting over with, they start playing like a team. "Nothing in the world could stop us now. Winning makes winning like money makes money, and we had power and pitching and speed, so much of it that if anybody done anything wrong nobody ever noticed. There was too much we were doing right. It was a club, like it should of been all year but never was but all of a sudden become" (p. 241).

The implications quickly extend, of course. Bruce, speculating on why a formerly hostile teammate is suddenly friendly to him, says, " 'Probably you told him or something.' . . . 'I never told a soul,' said I. 'Probably everybody be nice to you if they knew you were dying,' he said. 'Everybody knows everybody is dying,' I said. 'That is why people are nice. You all die soon enough, so why not be nice to each other?' " (p. 140).

Henry's words, of course, are only logic, not truth. In fact he *had* told the player, which *was* why he was being nice. When Henry tells Red, "Everybody knows they are dying," Red replies, "They do not act like they know it" (p. 207).

Most of the time, simply, they do not know it. But with death immediately present for them, they are brought together, the knowledge made lighter by sharing it. "It made me feel very sad. Yet I knew that some of the boys felt the same, and knowing it made me feel better. Not being alone with it any more was a great help, knowing that other boys knew, even if only a few, and you felt warm towards them, and you looked at them, and them at you, and you were both alive, and you might as well said, 'Ain't it something? Being alive I mean!' " (p. 212).

And, in some inexplicable way, the shared knowledge of mortality, which has made the men appreciate and take seriously their work and their lives and pulled them together into human fellowship, ends by making them value things beyond their own lives.

We see this paradoxical new morality in a very interesting scene. Henry had earlier sold Bruce a $50,000 insurance policy, and Katie, a high-class prostitute Bruce is infatuated with, has learned that he is dying and has agreed to marry him if he makes her (rather than his father) the beneficiary. Bruce is willing, but Henry keeps stalling on their request that he have the policy changed. Finally Katie tries to bribe Henry to change it, offering such things as money, or a lifetime pass to her establishment. " 'You will not be playing ball forever,' she said. 'You have a short life.' 'So do you,' I said. 'So does everybody.' 'Then why not live it up a little?' she said. 'Why worry so much about Pearson's old man?' 'I do not know,' I said, and that was true, for I did not. Do not ask me why you do not live it up all the time when dying is just around the corner, but you don't. You would think you would, but you don't. 'I don't know why,' I said" (p. 217).

VIII   *Final Assessment*

The novel has many kinds of excellence. I have been trying to show how tightly theme and action are intertwined, and this obtains down to the smallest details, such as Henry's selling everyone life insurance, and to Bruce a bigger policy than any of the others, and how this proves so feckless a hedge against their common mortality. The whole first scene of the book is a marvel of little details in the reordering of Henry's values as he moves from ignorance to the knowledge of death. Because of his recent financial troubles, no doubt, he had perhaps been giving too high a value to money. On the first page of the novel, he begins by refusing the collect call Bruce makes to him from the hospital. Next, he tells him he cannot go see him. " 'I cannot afford it,' I said. 'I am up to my ass in tax arrears.' This was the statement of a true rat" (p. 4), he quickly owns, but still only grumblingly agrees to go because he can try to sell insurance to some of the players living in Minnesota, and thereby call it a business trip and deduct his expenses. Even when he gets there he is briefly tempted into a flirtation with an airline stewardess, then thinks better of it; calls a player about insurance, in order to get his deduction; buys a heavy winter coat; has a leisurely dinner at a restaurant; and only then (sex, money, food, warmth having come first) goes to visit his friend in the hospital. He had not, of course, realized how serious Bruce was. Later, to show his reformation, when he gets the clause in his contract linking him and Bruce together, he quickly signs it, even though he might still have held out for more money.

Another excellence, as always in a Harris novel, is the humor, particularly in the interviews Dutch has with Henry where he is asking him searching questions, trying to trip him up and get to the bottom of what is going on. Henry makes up a number of elaborate stories to account for his being in Rochester, Minnesota:

"Well, Dutch," said I, "you will probably think I am a heel and all that, but there is this airline stewardess."
"What is her name?"
"Mary," I said.
"Mary what? Jones or Smith or Brown?"
"Mary Pistologlione," I said (p. 100).

Also fine is the developing character of Bruce, and, as in *The Southpaw*, the convincingly rendered baseball scenes. A single great weakness, it seems to me, is found in the scenes with Katie the whore, whose character is unconvincing. She apparently eats only in fancy restaurants and has girls of every race and color in her establishment, including stars of stage and screen, but charges only twenty dollars for her own services, a price tag which does not seem very high-class even for 1955. She is another version, I suppose, of Patricia Moors, the corrupting femme fatale, a trumped-up character who seems the more two-dimensional for all the real felt life around her.

Finally the book, for all that is good in it, does not come up to its predecessor. It is hard to put a finger on the reasons why, but perhaps it depends too much upon the earlier book; perhaps too much of the invention had already taken place in *The Southpaw*, and this book, doing many of the same fine things, still does not extend them enough, does not break enough new ground. Harris had misgivings himself about the book, thinking of it as a possible "evasion. I think I may have been anxious to repeat. In a way that book is a rewrite of an earlier book."[13]

IX   A Ticket for a Seamstitch

There might not have been a third baseball novel, except that the associate editors of *Life* wrote Harris and asked him especially for a new Henry Wiggen story. The thought of a large national audience and a considerable amount of money was no doubt very tempting. Harris wrote a tentative first version of his story for them, perhaps holding back a bit, fearful of what subjects might be too touchy for a national magazine. The editors sent it back, saying they liked it, but asking him to let himself go, say what he liked, expand the story to a novel if necessary. He did so, working fourteen hours a day on the story, "and when it was done I knew that I had done something I shall never quite do again, and my friends at *Life* knew what I had done and they sent it up—up to the man upstairs—and he said No."[14]

Instead of his story, *Life* published a bit of book-of-the-month-club hackwork by William Brinkley. Harris has written a rueful and amusing account of the affair in "Easy Does It Not," for Granville Hicks's *The Living Novel: A Symposium*. In the same piece he gives the plot of the novel:

A young lady [the "seamstitch," or seamstress of the title] writes to Henry Wiggen from "somewhere out West" to tell him that she will be in New York to watch the Mammoths play on July 4th. Henry is her hero. But Henry has a wife, and for this reason (he says) he attempts to transfer the young lady's affection from himself to Thurston Woods, inevitably called "Piney," a twenty-year-old catcher with a passion for women of the Hollywood type, fast motorcycles, and low-slung automobiles.

We follow the young lady's cross-country journey, wherein she is endangered but never quite violated (she says). She is delayed for a time at the Geographical Center of the United States Motel, whose owner's intentions toward her are ambiguous but who finally delivers her safely to New York. . . .

Piney Woods discovers, when the girl arrives, that she is no beauty. His dream has overshot reality. He begins to discover, however, that love and charm may reside even within a form less divine than Hollywood specifies (pp. 109 - 10).

The story had been commissioned for an early July issue of *Life*, so Harris arranged much of the action to climax on the Fourth of July. The young lady from out West will arrive on that day to see Wiggen pitch. On that day Henry will be trying for his sixteenth straight win, which will tie the record for consecutive wins and assure Henry's eventual entrance into baseball's Hall of Fame. A great deal of national imagery begins to gather about the Fourth of July date. For instance, Piney Woods, who in *Bang the Drum Slowly* had strummed "Streets of Laredo" on his guitar, appropriately the ballad of a boy dying young, throughout the present novel plays tunes out of a new book of patriotic hymns chorded for the guitar. The Mammoths' colors, it turns out, are red, white, and blue. Baseball, of course, is the "national pastime." The girl, traversing the entire country, stops at the Geographical Center of the United States Motel, which has forty-eight rooms (the number of states at that time), and so on.

None of these details, in my estimation, ever becomes organically integrated with the novel's chief action. What does work particularly nicely in the novel, it seems to me—though Harris does not allude to it in the plot summary he gives—is Henry's part in the action. If Piney Woods, the green rookie, lets his dreams overshoot reality ("Mind over matter" is his favorite expression), Henry, the veteran "old hand," is very close to letting certain kinds of reality stifle his dreams. If for Piney a young lady writing from out West must be ravishingly beautiful, to Henry, who gets fan letters by the ream, anyone writing must be just one more "cluck," like the thousands of clucks in the stands for whom he has nothing but contempt. Ultimately matter over mind will bring both of them, and the girl as well, to a more balanced position. For she has come across country trusting everyone, and though not everyone's intentions are as innocent as her own (when she puts up, midjourney, with the Queen City Cowboys, players keep knocking on her door late at night wishing to discuss baseball) she does arrive unscathed, only to find first of all that Henry has palmed her off on Piney, and Piney, after one look at her, has palmed her back onto Henry. She suddenly oscillates to the other extreme, calling all men, especially Piney, snakes. " 'No,' said I, 'lacking in experience and being a snake is 2 different things' " (p. 106).[15]

Before ever seeing her, Piney had drawn a picture of her looking
"like 40,000 stars of stage and screen" (58). The reality did not approach his fantasy. "Average," is Henry's assessment, "nothing
below average and nothing too much above, just exactly the
average kind of girl you bump into everywhere you turn" (p. 103).
A "cluck," in other words. He does the decent thing, however, taking her to dinner, to the automat where she has always wanted to
go. To his surprise, he enjoys himself, flooded with memories of
when he was a young rookie first come to the big-time and had
himself enjoyed eating at the automat. As he gets to know the girl,
she stops being an anonymous cluck and starts looking better. The
next day, in fact, "She looked better than she looked. A good sleep
always done wonders for her, she said, or maybe she only looked
better because once you hang with somebody awhile they look
better" (p. 111).

He makes his greatest concession when he actually goes up into
the stands and sits in a box with her while the first game of the
doubleheader is going on (he will try for his record pitching the second game). The people in the boxes behind them, unknown,
anonymous, therefore "clucks" to Henry, are making stupid comments about the game, and he is, as always, contemptuous of them.
But when the girl, the seamstress, makes stupid remarks, he patient-
ly explains to her what is going on.

For instance, when the opposing pitcher strikes out a Mammoth
player:

"He got the face of a thief and a moron," she said. . . .
"No," said I, "he is a fine and pleasant country boy throwing for
groceries. . . ."
I got a lot to learn" (p. 134).

They all have, and they all do. Henry, playing the part of the old
pro, had said of his forthcoming attempt at the record, "It is only a
baseball game. I won some and I lost some in my life. . . . After
all, I am libel to lose another ball game some day. You win and you
lose" (p. 93). But in fact when he pitches and loses, he admits to
feeling "lousy" (p. 138). It does mean something to him, and it
should. It turns out, in part, to be the insouciant Piney, a wonderful
comic character, who helps lose the game for him, because Piney is
much more involved with thinking about the girl than the game.
Everyone, in short, has his mind somewhere other than where it

ought to be. But by the end Piney, forced by Henry, has taken the girl to dinner and had a "pretty good" time (p. 142), though he and the girl are both bored with the automat by now and are ready for something less legendary, more solid.

A Ticket for a Seamstitch, like *Bang the Drum Slowly*, is full of fine things but, again, is perhaps too much of a repetition. And perhaps it suffers from being an inflated short story. It seems in the end rather slight.

In fact, Harris wrote no more baseball novels and ceased to create semiliterate narrators for his stories. Even this last work, as I have suggested, might not have been written had it not been specifically commissioned. Harris had already finished a novel which was published in the same year as *A Ticket for a Seamstitch*, but one which was to take his art in a new direction.

CHAPTER 4

Something About a Soldier

THIS novel did not make the critical stir that *The Southpaw*, or later, *Wake Up, Stupid*, did, nor did it find as many
readers. And yet it seems to me the finest of Harris's works.[1] The
story is simple. In 1944 seventeen-year-old Jacob Epstein enters the
army, and is sent to Georgia for basic training—"one hundred and
twenty-one days [that] had everlastingly shaped and formed him"
(p. 5).[2] His comfortable early life in Perkinsville had sheltered him
from social reality, but once in Georgia, a witness to racial discrimination and to the hard lot of the poor, he becomes a social ac-
tivist, even, briefly, a Communist agent. He also meets a young girl
named Joleen who feels that, instead of embracing first capitalism
and then communism, Jacob should give up abstractions and start
embracing her, as a more tangible object for his love of humanity.
Captain Dodd, his company commander, takes an interest in Jacob,
liking his fresh intelligence and eagerness for life. Dodd also likes
Joleen, and having a mature man's knowledge of women, is soon
taking her regularly to a nearby hotel, at a time when Jacob has not
dared kiss her goodnight. To her surprise, Joleen finds herself quite
capable of loving both of them equally.

As the basic-training period comes to an end, Dodd, who knows
that ultimately youth belongs with youth, also knows that the bat-
talion is heading for certain death in combat and he begins devising
ways to save Jacob:

> Wouldn't you like not to die? You're sure to die.
> I don't take such a defeatist attitude, sir.
> Bullets go where they're sent, said Dodd, like soldiers or Fascists or Com-
> munists. They don't have attitudes.
> Everybody has attitudes.
> Bullets, goddam it, you stupid goddam fool. Bullets. Bullets don't have
> attitudes.
> Yes sir.

62

If you missed a lot of bedchecks you wouldn't die. If you went far away and didn't come back you wouldn't die. Do you hear what I say? (pp. 109 - 10—dialogue in this novel is written without quotation marks).

This solution might have been unthinkable to Jacob, but then he gets word his close friend has been killed in action, a friend who had been voted in high school Most Likely to Succeed (Jacob had been voted Most Brilliant). "He had great accomplishments planned," Jacob moans. "You next," says Dodd (pp. 119 - 20), and Jacob does run for it now, walking out on his platoon, being picked up later by MPs near his home, being placed in isolation in the army stockade, where he goes on a hunger strike. Dodd, as his last act before being shipped overseas to die with the rest of the battery, gets him a psychiatric discharge.

Jacob had acted spontaneously, emotionally, but the philosophical rightness of his action is clear in every event of the novel. Nevertheless, it is not until fifteen years later that Jacob, who at first had felt shame and disgrace, begins to see this.

In time, however, considerations of patriotic duty were replaced by a new remorse: he had failed, not his country, but certain men, and it was this that began to seem to Jacob to be his greatest sin. Its burden upon him became heavier and not lighter. He asked himself, as time passed, What men did I fail? Could I really have saved them? What are their names? What is the color of their eyes? They must bear a name, he thought, or they are but an abstraction, and a man cannot betray an abstraction. A man may betray a priest but he cannot betray a church, a student but not a school, a woman but not women. So that, as Jacob pondered, his country eventually vanished, and only Dodd remained, and Jacob knew that he had betrayed only one man, Dodd (p. 2).

Dodd had died to save him for love. He is freed now to go find Joleen, who, not knowing of his discharge, had lived all fifteen years thinking he had been killed with the rest.

I   *The Novel of Personal Experience*

The immediate difference between *Something About a Soldier* (1957) and the three baseball novels preceding it is that here Harris is writing in his own language about a character rather like himself undergoing something very close to his own experience.[3] The result, oddly perhaps, has been to liberate him. I have already suggested that Henry's semiliterate language was becoming more and more of a trap for Harris. This novel, like the earlier ones, is full of strong characters, of wacky dialogue, but this time the various characters' speaking voices are subtly discriminated, and behind the action is Harris's fine narrative style and the delicate wit, the quiet irony of his commentary. The language, fleshed out in this way, shows Harris at his best.

A longish example may show the quality of it. Here is young Jacob (who had earlier changed his name from Epstein to Epp in order to get a job) getting on the train to Georgia, skimming through a *Life* magazine, still unaware of the war nerves building up around him:

Before boarding a train, he paid ten cents for a copy of LIFE (bearing a coverphoto entitled Ear Muffs showing a beautiful girl with earmuffs

In the great days after victory, we may get flying flivvers, tireless tubes, and plastic bathtubs. But despite all the wonders of
Sirs: Usually correct in scientific matters, I believe LIFE, in the article on skip-bombing (LIFE, Nov. 15), has made an error which should be obvious
There's a Christmas rush on telephone wires, too. Help keep war-crowded circuits clear. War needs the wires—even on holidays.

to any person
having taken an elementary course in physics. I refer to the caption: "As bomb is slowed slightly by gravity and air resistance . . ." According to the laws of physics as taught here at Princeton
Give her a War Bond and you give her the best . . . Give her a Hoover and you give her

requesting that, when Jacob has finished reading his copy of LIFE, he cooperate with the War Production Board by sharing it with a friend or neighbor

My Harvel Watch Withstood the Shock of that shaking Fool Machine Gun. Here is an excerpt from an actual. . . .

and a backcover photo of Sergeant Tommy It's Always Camels with Me comparing them critically, taking a T-Zone Test, smoking Camel Choice Quality Turkish & Domestic Blend).

While he read he whistled between his teeth There'll Always Be An England, and when he finished reading he offered the magazine to the soldier beside him, to whom he had introduced himself, but who had not responded in kind. This struck Jacob as unmannerly, not in the true spirit of camaraderie. Were they not brothers in arms, even if not yet in their soldiersuits?

Assuming, as he easily did, that the soldier beside him was Irish, Jacob thought it appropriate to describe in some detail, listing affirmative points on his fingers, a debate he had engaged in in his junior year at Perkinsville High School (I mean the year, said Jacob, before I was unanimously elected co-captain) upon the subject *Resolved:* Irish Neutrality Endangers Allied Power. The Irishman could not have been less interested.

Aren't you Irish?

What the hell you ask so many questions for? Here's your book back and stop talking for once.

It's a free country.

For the rich and the Jews, said the Irishman.

I would differ with you on that, said Jacob, because I only recently read a study showing—

What it showed he never said, for the Irishman turned in his seat and swung roundhouse with his open hand, and Jacob saw the hand coming and raised his own, and his own knuckles were driven backward into one lens of his eyeglasses. He was astonished.

Jacob did not return the blow. . . .

He examined the split lens. It was a nine-dollar lens. It's not the money, he thought. Nine dollars was little enough to him whose father earned twenty thousand dollars a year, nor was it even the inconvenience of seeing all the world through a split lens. Yet he was disheartened. And in this moment he resolved to reassume his original and long-time name, the name he had been given at birth, and to answer to no other (pp. 10 - 13).

Although I have quoted this as an example of Harris's mature prose, the passage (as indeed almost any passage) will also serve to demonstrate his "absolute economy and fierce compression"[4] as well, a thematic density going beyond the baseball novels. This is the second way writing about his own experience liberated him. In the baseball novels a great deal of space is taken up with baseball itself, games played, position in the league, and so on. Quite properly so, and some of the baseball scenes, or scenes set up by baseball, are masterful. One of the great scenes in *The Southpaw* is the final speech of fatherly advice given Henry by Mike Mulrooney just before Henry is sent up to the majors.[5] Everything in the novel has led up to that particular scene, and Harris brings it off perfectly. Yet what seems remarkable is how completely the scene stays within the novel. Polonius's speech to Laertes ("Neither a borrower nor a lender be") is in the same order of speeches of fathers to sons about to be launched into life, but his is a general-purpose speech, suitable for any father to any son, readily capable of application in our own lives. Mike's speech ("Watch everything Sad Sam does on

the field, but off the field don't have anything to do with him.") has
no reference to anything outside that particular novel. At this point,
interestingly, the novel begins to achieve the sort of purity certain
poetry aims at. However, the baseball novels have their thematic
concerns as well, creating a split. At times even in *The Southpaw*,
the most perfectly realized of the three, the themes (pacifism, racial
prejudice, what constitutes the successful life) can seem extrinsic,
tacked on. Contrarily in *Bang the Drum Slowly* and *A Ticket for a
Seamstitch*, it is the baseball scenes themselves which seem to in-
trude occasionally on what we feel the books are trying to be about.

There is no such split in *Something About a Soldier*. Unlike
Henry, Jacob has no speech patterns or tastes or professional interests differing from Harris's, so that he need not be elaborately
and page-by-consuming-page invented and given verisimilitude.
Jacob differs from Harris at most in degree. He is bright ("his IQ
never fitted any curve"—p. 77), literate ("he could easily read a
book a day"—p. 2), fluent (a prize-winning high-school debater),
but also a very young, sheltered seventeen. For theme, the novel
deals with that central concern of Harris's, the consequences of
believing that the abstraction Society is more valuable than the con-
creteness of individual men. The novel does not approach its theme
indirectly through a story about baseball. It confronts it directly:
Jacob and other individual human beings are inducted into the
army and trained to give up their lives to destroy that abstraction
Evil in order to save that abstraction The World.

The quotation begins with Jacob skimming *Life*, as we all do (or
did), looking at pictures, half reading captions, glancing through
letters, ads—but it is more than a virtuoso passage showing the
curve of a speed reader's attention. The glimpses of *Life* also serve
to give us the official American position at its most superficial, with
its bland statements about "the great days after victory." Jacob's
generation of young men will still have time to go out and get killed
before those great days come. The ads, all with a patriotic slogan or
two before going into their pitch, are at first comic, then sinister,
underlining the close connections between making money and making war. And we see the intellectuals' collusion in the war with the
letter writer from Princeton being interested only in the technical
accuracy of the skip bomb and not its moral implications.

Something About a Soldier is an education novel, just as *The
Southpaw* was, and at this early stage it is indicative that Jacob is
nowhere critical of the official picture of "life," if nowhere, either,
very attentive to it. Indeed, with Sergeant Tommy in mind, Jacob

in his effort to grow up quickly goes out later and buys some Camels. And in cooperation with the War Production Board he turns to share the magazine with his neighbor.

It is here that the comfortable abstractions are confronted with their first dose of individual reality. Jacob's neighbor does not want the magazine, does not want Jacob's neighborliness. A poor boy, and thus closer to the truth of their situation than Jacob (they are, after all, being sent off to kill or be killed), the nervous inductee responds to Jacob's calm certainty by striking him. Later the company mail clerk will also lash out at him, just as Henry Wiggen, in *The Southpaw*, is violently attacked by a hopeful rookie who is not making the grade ("Just some pitiful moron that is losing his nerve"[6]). Jacob begins to see "all the world through a split lens," a situation that worsens a little later when, tired of explaining to everyone how the lens got cracked "he carefully removed the split lens from its frame, thus rendering the damage less conspicuous but producing the odd effect of a landscape divided, a near world and a far world. His head began to ache" (p. 21). His vision from the far world of abstraction had told him his neighbor would show "a true spirit of camaraderie. Were they not brothers in arms, even if not yet in their soldiersuits?" But his near vision has already begun to show him real "life" is much more complicated. Wearing uniforms to fight some official but abstract Evil, far from uniting individuals, would only dehumanize them. But early in his career Jacob is mis reading all the signs. He decides the misunderstanding is his own fault, resulting from his trying to pass himself off as Epp, a Gentile, rather than Epstein, a Jew: "When people don't know what you are they say things they wouldn't say if they knew what you were" (p. 15). He is being naïve. Jacob's fault throughout is his belief that good sense and the logic of debate will prevail in the world. He has conveniently forgotten that he had had to change his name in the first place "to apply at Stickles Brothers" (p. 15). Nor had he particularly noticed when a black classmate of his, a fellow member of the debating team, was separated from him in New York to be sent to racially segregated army training. He only remembered the black student's skillful defense of Free Trade.

II *Jacob's Education*

Jacob's education proceeds by wide pendulum swings. "My trouble always was, I get these enthusiasms" (p. 120). At the start, as would be expected of a boy "whose father earned twenty thousand dollars a year," he is a capitalist blithely enough on his way to "put an end to evil" (p. 17). His father is a "financier," he naïvely boasts (a pawnbroker, actually), and he has numbers of daydreams in which he interrogates Hitler, allowing him to smoke one last Camel before sending him out to his execution. When he has his first date with Joleen, a dance at the union hall where her father works (a subversive union, at that), "the building itself was wooden and old and the stairways creaked, these signs of decrepitude confirming him in his belief that the occupants were shabby in intent. Affluent organizations with nothing to be ashamed of would not hide themselves away in such a structure; great works could be carried forward only in great places of marble and steel, as at Stickles Brothers in New York City" (p. 47). He patronizes Joleen's working-class father, and disapproves of the union support of Roosevelt, who was "surely not *Jacob's* president" (p. 48).

At the same time he has been so exemplary a soldier, so letter-perfect in every article of uniform, bed-making, drill, as to be un-animously nicknamed by the troops, "Chickenshit."

But his first awareness of racial discrimination in the South, and—mainly—his reading about the Civil War, begins to change the direction of his thinking. "He lay crying over the hanging of John Brown and the assassination of Abraham Lincoln. . . . There now existed a new dimension to himself. Heretofore he had been a Jew and an American, and now he was also a Northerner, and he was therefore, now, suddenly, larger than he had been" (p. 56). But larger only in abstractions (he has yet to meet his first black socially). Nevertheless, he takes action. He steals a packet of labels from the first sergeant's desk and begins pasting them up in promi-nent places with statements like "THEY SHOULD HAVE LET THE SOUTH SECEDE" and "ABOLISH RACIAL SEGREGATION IN THE ARMED FORCES."

He argues with the yawning men of his platoon that John Brown should never have been hanged: "In my opinion he was one of the ten greatest men that ever lived.

"The greatest man that ever lived, said Private Atterbury, is the man that hands me my discharge" (p. 58).

Although Jacob has not yet achieved so personal a view of history, he becomes less good as a soldier, even losing his nickname, and realizes "how parochial he once had been. Whereas he had once felt himself to be, because he was a Jew, oppressed, he now knew an op-posite and more terrible emotion: he was no longer oppressed but oppressor, persecutor, no longer of the minority but of the majority, no longer weak but shamefully strong" (p. 61). He decides "he would be neither oppressed nor oppressor, so now his heart renounced killing equally with dying" (p. 62).

He holds this new position for only a short time. Nathan, a radical member of the radical union Joleen and her father belong to, politicizes him. He calls him Jacob "who loves capitalism but under capitalism must change his name. Oh well, it is only a few Jews put to the trouble."

It'll be Epstein again, said Jacob.
But can the Negro change back their skin? Oh well, a few Negroes. Capitalism will solve it all. We will abolish segregation in your army and exclusion in my Union by printing stickers for the walls, and we will paste them over the pisspots, and that will solve it all. Your house is on fire and you call the firemen, and the firemen paste stickers on the wall, ABOLISH FIRE IN JACOB'S HOUSE.
You're oversimplifying, said Jacob.
Hitler the madman is loose in Europe murdering Jews and attacking the socialist sixth of the world. Paste stickers to the wall, ABOLISH HITLER THE MADMAN (p.89).

Jacob yields to a superior debater. He joins the Communist party (his membership card going in his wallet next to his membership card in the Young Republicans club) and, forgetting his recent vow of pacifism, pastes up stickers (since he can think of no more direct action) saying "DEMAND THE SECOND FRONT" (p. 94)—asking, in other words, for the Americans to invade Europe. It is on this second front that all the young men in Jacob's platoon will soon be killed.

What Jacob does not realize is that he has come full circle. Fighting the war for communism is really no different from fighting the war for capitalism. The parallels are strong. When he worked for Stickles Brothers he had "delivered sealed documents to other firms" (p. 47). As a Communist, he has the same job of conveying, in sealed envelopes, secret messages. At Stickles Brothers he was called Epp, as an agent he is called "Comrade," a name that had seduced him at first but finally is as depersonalizing as his Gentile name. When he meets his contact on a dark street:

Comrade . . . I can't see your face, he said.
You ain't concerned with the face, you only concerned with this envelope. . . .

What's in them?
In the envelopes?
Yes.
I don't know. It ain't my business and it ain't yours (p.94).

For the giant abstractions on either side, he is only an anonymous cipher. At this point Jacob's friends understand him better than he understands himself. Dodd asks Joleen:

Is he in love with you?
He loves the world, she said.
Impossible, said Dodd.
Or anyhow that's what he claims, she said. He talks a lot.
   . . . I think love is one man and one woman, not words and flags and printed promises. I think Jacob's a liar if he says he loves the world.
He's not, she said. Or if he is he doesn't mean to be.
I think he might love somebody someday, said Dodd, if he lives that long, which he will, if I can swing it" (p. 70).

III   *The Word and the Spirit*

"He talks a lot," Joleen says. The verbal facility, the logical mind, are what push him to abstractions, blocking his very real human emotions. The question of logical debate versus the response of the heart is itself presented, in the novel, as a debate. On one side, and brooding over the novel, is the Union cannon in the square of his home town, with its inscription "ULTIMA RATIO REGUM," the final argument of despots. On the other side stands Joleen. When the inexperienced Jacob asks her permission for a kiss, "Kiss me, she said. Love me. Don't talk about it or it gets away" (p. 102).

In between is the champion debater Jacob, with his firm belief in the Word. It is interesting that his first turn to pacifism is nonverbal. "His heart renounced killing equally with dying. But this he could not express. . ." (p. 62). It is Nathan, no mean debater himself (despite what Jacob sees as "his innocence of the rules of debate, his *post hoc* fallacies and his *ad hominem* fallacies and his Invalid Generalizations") who first seriously shakes his belief in debate. "Jacob had writhed for long, it seemed, among questions which had two and three and four sides, and never any answers. I won the debates, said Jacob, and what did I win when I won, only cups and medals, and everything was the same, no changes and no improvements, and everybody hating everybody just the same. I hate nobody" (p. 93).

But Nathan has turned him away from the Word that kills only to present him with another word:

"Don't you hate capitalism? said Nathan.

"Well yes, said Jacob, I guess I always hated capitalism all right" (p. 93), and he ends up demanding the second front.

The solution to the debate, when it comes, is appropriately sublogical, nonverbal. Jacob, "ambitious to love, and love only" (p. 4), turns his back, and walks away from the army.

IV   *The Novel as Parable*

The novel is closely based on Harris's personal experience, and yet how effortlessly it becomes universal, how quickly the young man, though so special, comes to stand for all young men! Contributing to this is the novel's symbolism, understated and ancillary, but worth examining. Captain Dodd, who arranged the medical discharge for Jacob, thus preserving him for the future, and for Joleen (whom Dodd calls "Love"), can be seen as a Christ figure. Such a reading is not insisted on by Harris, but is certainly possible. His name, to begin with, rhymes with God; he is, calculations within the book allow us to figure, about thirty-three, the age at which he is killed immediately upon going overseas; by profession his father was a judge and he himself "used to law" (p. 69).

Jacob "often imagined himself the victim of an obscure law" (p. 26): the significance of his biblical name is obvious, the promise of future life about to be senselessly sacrificed by the older generation. Dodd at the last moment intervenes and saves him—indeed dies so that he may live. Through rather broad double meaning, his role as creator is seen when Joleen confesses to Jacob:

"He made me a woman. Do you know what I mean?"

". . . He made me a man, too, or at least he saved me from being a dead boy" (p.173).

V   *The Argument against War*

The arguments against war, however, are not simply translated into an easy Christian symbolism. As I have said before, Harris is a harder-line pacifist than most of us, opposing even such seemingly justifiable wars as that against Hitler. His view comes down to the central notion of the value of the individual over the abstraction of his society. Jacob, practicing against straw men with his bayonet,

outwardly shouting *Jap bastard, German Bastard,* inwardly has misgivings. "While it might, he felt, be agreeable or desirable to kill a
German who had earlier killed Jews, it was somewhat excessive to
kill the first German he met without inquiring into that *particular*
German's views. But would there be time to inquire?" (p. 115).

There is a quiet but unanswerable insistence in the novel that
war—like debate—solves nothing, and we are reminded throughout
the novel of many wars; of the Civil War, which had not ended
racial intolerance; of "the big war," in which his father had lost a
leg. "And for what? To make the world safe for what? The war to
end war" (p. 145). When, fifteen years after the central events of
the novel, Jacob goes to the registry of the dead to look up Dodd
and the members of his platoon, to find them all dead, the clerk
asks him what war he wants the registers for. "For the last war, said
Jacob. For the Second World War, he amended, remembering that
that war was now no longer the last [the Korean War Having in-
tervened]" (p. 145), had solved no more than any other.

When he is on a hunger strike in the army stockade, refusing to
cooperate any further with the "War Production Board," even in
his delirium he comes to a firm belief that he will survive and be
valued: "Because I, after all, serve my country, because I
perpetuate and keep alive and do not permit to die the idea of stopping fighting even when everybody else is fighting" (p.147).

"The wars would end," Jacob concludes, "when men stopped
fighting them" (p. 145).

I have said I believe *Something About a Soldier* is the best of
Harris's novels. I have tried to locate its excellence in its language,
and in its basic story, which is so perfectly chosen that it allows
Harris to say everything he wants to say, and yet retains the purity
and simplicity of a traditional fable. But there is in addition a very
logical reason for its success. Harris's books, almost without exception, have been either novels or autobiographies, and these two
forms have at times nearly merged: the novels tending to be
autobiographical, the autobiographies tending to be novelistic. My
own feeling—and the thesis of the present book—is that Harris's
significant work is in the novel, and that the autobiographies,
though interesting in their own right, readable, and no doubt
therapeutic for the author, are minor. Writing fact, Harris loses the
poetic power of fiction. Yet his fictions have an opposite problem.

Making himself the "disguised person" in his fictions has led him into the sometimes unnecessary complications which are caused, for instance, by his disguising himself as a baseball player. In one book only, *Something About a Soldier*, he is writing a novel, and yet the novel is directly about himself. The combination exactly suited his needs and his talents.

CHAPTER 5

Definition in Two Keys: Wake Up, Stupid, *and* The Goy

H ARRIS'S next two novels, *Wake Up, Stupid* (1959), and, after a
long gap, *The Goy* (1970), are two versions of the same story.
The first novel, fresh and amiable, was a popular success for Harris.[1]
But Harris then turned from the novel, and his next major works
were in the drama *(Friedman & Son,* 1963) and autobiography
(Mark the Glove Boy, 1964, and *Twentyone Twice,* 1966). When
more than a decade later he returned to the novel, it was to write a
dark version of *Wake Up, Stupid,* with all of the first novel's
possibilities for violence and ugliness realized, instead of pulled
back from at the last moment.

I Wake Up, Stupid

Several of Harris's past approaches to the novel are brought
together in *Wake Up, Stupid.* In the first place, he has linked his
athlete hero with his intellectual hero: the protagonist, Lee
Youngdahl, is a college teacher who had been a promising
professional boxer. In the second place, this is once more a coming-
of-age novel. Youngdahl had given up boxing and turned to
teaching when he began feeling too much sympathy for his op-
ponents in the ring (so much sympathy that he forgot to keep his
guard up). But he is dissatisfied with being a teacher. Teaching does
not seem to be enough. Life is passing him by. So he sets out to be a
Broadway playwright, a Harvard professor, a great romantic lover,
and to manage a prize-fighter (commercial success, scholarly
renown, sexual freedom and physical expression). In the course of
the novel he is "defined," as one after another of these goals proves
illusory and he returns to his teaching life at least slightly more at
peace with himself. No man can live all possible lives; the one he
has chosen is sufficient.

74

II *The Structure of* Wake Up, Stupid

The structure of the novel is a sort of culmination of Harris's interest in exploiting the relationship between life and art, between the writer and the written document. It is an epistolary novel.

In an ordinary novel the actions and speeches of men are transposed into words on a printed page. But with a novel which is composed of a series of letters, one of the middlemen between art and life has been eliminated, for letters in real life are already written documents. There is no physical difference between a real and a fictional letter. [2]

Not that in practice this makes a great deal of difference. Our imaginations trained in the conventions of reading fiction, our disbelief suspended, we readily invigorate the written words of whatever kind with the color and sound and movement of life. And in any case, at the very moment we are believing in the lives of Harris's characters, we still know they are characters in a novel, and we believe in them in the special way we believe in all fiction, which means that with no sense of inconsistency we can also more or less consciously enjoy the imposition of form on what we are reading.

It is not, then, to be more realistic that Harris seeks to remove some of the barriers between life and fiction. (In addition to imitating letters, which are written documents, he has also introduced into this novel, as into other of his novels, actual documents, real news clippings, real religious tracts, which he intermingles with the fictional life of his characters, bringing both actual and imagined lives under the same artistic control.) Harris has written: "For a writer who has advanced beyond a certain stage of his life, the work itself is experience."[3] In other words, the time and thought consumed in writing is so much a part of Harris's life that his life and his fiction literally interpenetrate, and this is the case with Lee Youngdahl, who in this respect is one more disguise for Harris. The structure becomes thematic, meaning and form interfusing; for the life Lee is trying to define, to accept or reject, is the life of the serious writer, and it is in the process of writing about his struggles that he resolves them. Structure also becomes an expression of character, for Youngdahl, like Harris, must write a little every day: "I am vowed to write each night at least one useful letter to a friend or enemy. I must write a little something every night, as a fighter punches the bag a little every day" (p. 7).[4]

This is not to say Harris does not make the epistolary form work

for him in a number of other ways as well. When Samuel Richardson first perfected the form, writing *Pamela* and *Clarissa,* he was
quite aware of the advantages of writing "to the moment," when
the outcome of events was still in suspense, when the person writing
had no more idea than the reader what was coming next. Harris certainly exploits this technique and many others of Richardson's, using to dramatic effect the time-lag, the discontinuity, the subjectivi-
ty, of letters.

To give a trivial but amusing example of one way Harris uses the
structure: back in the days before our present liberalism, Harris (he
once told me) had to fight with editors and publishers to be allowed
to use the obscenities he thought were the natural expressions of
some of his characters. We see this in the "SPECIAL WARNING
TO ALL READERS!!!" Henry Wiggen posts at the beginning of
The Southpaw, explaining that Pop, in this case, had made him
clean up the book a bit. " 'I can swallow the 'damns' and the 'hells'
and even worse,' said he, 'but as for the 'f———s' they are simply
too much for my eyes to bear. I wish you would blank them in,
Hank.' " Aaron then gives Pop a sentence out of *Tom Jones* to read:
"D——n un, what a sly b——ch 'tis."

> "Read it out loud," said Aaron to Pop.
> Pop read out loud as follows: "Damn un, what a sly bitch 'tis."
> "Ho ho," said Aaron, "you have blanked out the blanks in your mind"
> (unpaged, from the front of the book).

Nonetheless Henry gives in, and blanks out the worst obscenities.
The problem is evidently still present for Harris in writing *Wake
Up, Stupid,* and so he has another joke at his expurgator's expense.
Lee corresponds throughout the book with his nearly illiterate
literary agent, whose typewriter appears to be missing the letter
"f." After several f-less letters ("Have your typewriter fixed, you
phool," Lee demands [p. 3].), he tells Lee the joke about the
married man spending a night in a hotel with another man's wife.
They are both so remorse stricken at deceiving their spouses that
"they cry and cry and uck and uck" (p. 177).

At other points, Harris exploits the discontinuity of letters. We
live our life first, and then we write about it afterwards in letters,
but we do not necessarily write about it fully, or in proper sequence,
so reading only letters can at times be like hearing only one side of a
phone conversation. At the beginning of the novel, Lee has just

finished a play he had been working on for the past year. He gives it
to his friend Paul Purdy, who is going to have the university players
perform it. Rehearsals, in fact, have already begun. Suddenly, out
of the blue, Lee writes a brief letter to this close friend saying he is
instantly withdrawing the play, and if that causes a lot of inconvenience "that is the way things are" (p. 134). The letter drops
like a thunderbolt into the action, and it is not for several letters
more that we are given any explanation. We recall the brief letter in
Richardson's *Clarissa,* in which Lovelace writes to his friend Belford
that the rape has been committed, and we must wait hundreds of
pages before we find out what happened.

Harris also employs the natural time-lag of letters to achieve interesting thematic statements. In a letter to a friend, Lee jokingly
says that a mutual friend of theirs, a harebrained pilot, has crashed
and killed himself while performing some foolish stunt. The letter is
a fairly transparent invention, but we later learn that the friend has
taken it seriously and written an agonized letter of condolence to
the pilot's wife. By this time Lee is writing to the first friend about
some quite different matter, when he receives a reply from the
friend who is furious with him for joking about so serious a matter.
Lee writes back that, as an artist, he is concerned with general, not
particular, truth; that given the way their pilot friend behaves, it is
only a matter of time before he literally kills himself, so Lee's letter,
an artistic creation, is true in everything except for perhaps the
technical matter of timing.[5]

The next thing we hear is that the pilot actually has been killed.
Lee tells his friend, who replies, "Sure" (p. 213). Having believed
the probable fiction, he is not prepared to believe the too timely
fact. The ramifications here for life and art, for truth and fiction, for
the actual and probable, are almost endless.

III *The Options*

Lee Youngdahl has worked thirteen months without interruption
on his play. Now that it is finished, in the time that is suddenly on
his hands, he finds himself—partly, no doubt, a result of "post-
partum exhaustion" (p. 5)—dissatisfied with his life. He feels with
some justification that a man with his energy and charm, his personal attractiveness, his physical, intellectual, and artistic abilities,
must be capable of almost anything. His life as a serious writer who
must teach to earn his living begins to seem like a pretty small ex-

pression of his vast potential. In the course of the novel he begins to explore some larger options.

Just as in *The Southpaw*, the characters he encounters represent and become finally comments upon these various options. And just as in *The Southpaw*, that other group of characters, the protagonist's personal friends, wait, with decreasing patience, for him to see at last what they have seen from the beginning.

A. *Commercial Success*

Lee (like Harris himself) is a novelist of modest but respectable reputation, a serious writer with a serious audience, best known for a novel about a professional boxer, *The Hard Puncher*, which (just like one of Harris's novels) is about to have the dubious honor of being dramatized on national television. Although Lee is properly contemptuous of the fame he achieves through this medium, he may have been slightly corrupted after all. The "four pound play in one marathon act" which he has just completed, and given to his friend Paul Purdy, the drama professor at his school, to have the university perform, he now also sends off to his literary agent, Abner Klang, as a possible route "of escape from this wretched profession" (pp. 3 - 5).

Lee has to remind Abner that it is a play he has sent him: "there is no point in submitting it to Reader's Digest or Ring magazine or The Year's Best Crossword Puzzles. . . . Try to discard your absurd notions of where 'the top' is. You might try, first, the man who produced Paul Purdy's play" (p. 3). This man is a serious, small, off-Broadway producer, but perhaps there is already a bit of corruption here in Lee wanting the same success in the drama (not his primary form) as his friend[6] who specializes in it—"desiring this man's art and that man's scope." But Abner quickly replies that there is no money off-Broadway, and instead submits the play to a big-money-making Broadway producer. Lee, instead of objecting, at once plans a trip out to New York to meet this producer.

Abner, with his poor grammar and his single-minded notions for turning literature into cash, with his own creative endeavor limited to telling f-less jokes, is a comic grotesque. So are the other hacks whom Lee begins to associate with as he enters commercial literature. Victor Wenk, also illiterate, who is doing the adaptation of *The Hard Puncher* for television, keeps writing to him asking him to help with speeches for the characters which will explain to the audience what they are doing.[7] Harry Searle, successful writer of a soap-opera series, invites Lee to join The Dollar A Word Club. "Our meetings are quite informal. We exchange market tips, eat heartily. . . . It is quite a profitable experience in all ways. A number of our members, based on something heard or overheard, have gone away from our meetings with ideas for big sales" (p. 44).

An important constituent of these characters is a conscious or unconscious contempt for their audience. Searle smugly confesses to Lee that he is not even writing the soap opera that makes him $20,-000 a year. He is just dragging out scripts from eight or nine years ago, typing them up afresh, and sending them in. "Nobody the wiser. People are so damn stupid it's unbelievable. In my opinion, one of the best things that could ever happen was somebody come along and drop the atom bomb on them and get it over with" (p. 108). Lee, who has been having fun with Searle in several ways, responds by writing, using the voice and spelling of his mother, to the soap-opera sponsors, saying she and her friends will stop buying all the products the program advertises if they keep on fobbing off all those old programs on them.

Victor Wenk keeps writing to him for help in getting the speech of the referee right at the beginning of the fight. Lee finally answers him with a typical Harris lecture to "dramatize:"

Hard Puncher and Irishman come out of the corner, presumably for instructions, "at bell."

What bell? Is there a fire? Is it time for church? Is school out? Did it ever occur to you to go watch a prize-fight and attempt to link for yourself the pattern of bells to action?

Referee tells them that if anybody is knocked down he must be up by the count of ten.

Why? Don't they know? Do you mean to tell me they are professional boxers and they *don't know?* Impossible. I can't believe it, and nobody else will believe it either. My mother knows it. Every child in the nation knows it.

Hard Puncher says, "Let's start the fight and not waste any more time."

Why? In the novel he says "Let's start." Everybody knows what is to be started, and why he wants to start it. That's why they're there—to fight. They're not there to play chess, or they wouldn't be wearing boxing gloves. . . . Do not use more words than your characters need. Allow your characters to talk only to each other, not to some un-named unknown, invisible, imaginary, remote, and abstract "viewer." This "viewer," for all you know, is smarter than you are.

In Utah we say, "actions speak louder than words." This is the principle of drama. Not to believe in this principle is to show contempt for the human mind. Contempt for the human mind is Communistic and Fascistic, where the words contradict the action. Communism and Fascism are un-American. So straighten up (pp. 154 - 55).

Lee's characteristic injunction to "straighten up," just like the "wake up, stupid!" he has been known to shout at students, keeps coming back to Lee himself. He must face the fact that to enjoy popular success with his writing, he must align himself with these people and their attitudes. We remember Harris's experience in trying to write fiction for *Life:* "I see that a magazine like *Life* objects less to controversial subject matter than to difficult style. *Not irreverence, but craftsmanship, dismays the editors of mass media.*"

Lee now undergoes the same experience. When he gets to New York and meets Enright, the big-money producer, "Enright had a play doctor with him. 'Who's sick?' I said" (p. 189).

The "play doctor" complains that not enough things are explained in the play. Lee suggests introducing into the play "a handyman who at intervals will say, 'You mean . . . ?' " (p. 199) He then goes to see some of Enright's successful money-making plays.

The curtain rises on a very elaborate set, wherein we discover a mother and a daughter and a son. The mother explains to the son that she is his mother. The mother explains to the daughter that she (the mother) is her (the daughter's) mother. The son and the daughter explain to each other that they are brother and sister. They then explain to each other that father has for some years been in a madhouse. A psychiatrist arrives and explains that he is an old friend of the family. . ." (p. 207).

Of another Enright play, which might have had some nice ideas in it before the play doctor got hold of it, Lee observes, "Abner cautions me . . . not to squander my sympathies upon the man whose idea has been sacrificed, for he has become very rich" (pp. 200 - 201).

B.   Scholarly Renown

At the same time that he sends off his play, he begins to flirt with a second option. He writes to his scholarly friend Harold Rosenblatt (currently at Yale doing research): "Did I tell you of my Harvard offer? Of course I shall not go, but it is a mouse with which to tease the local cats: dare Mr. Gamble let me be dropped if it be known

that Harvard wants me?" (p. 6). He is up for tenure, so this is no
doubt a consideration. And no doubt, too, he is hoping to impress
his friend Harold, who, admiring him in other ways, may not have
much regard for him as a scholar. But the idea is teasing him as
well. His very next letter is to a friend at Harvard. "Once upon a
time you expressed the thought that Harvard might want me if I
want it, or her, or him, or them. Tell me now what you think" (p.
8). His friend writes back that he and other "youngdahlites" there
will begin working on the matter at once. He asks Lee to send a *vita*
"with emphasis upon your Boswell scholarship, some de-emphasis
of your popular articles, perhaps light mention of fiction. . ." (p.
42).

At a moment of crisis in the middle of the book, Lee fires off a
telegram to Harold saying, "I HAVE RESIGNED EFFECTIVE JUNE TO
ACCEPT AT HARVARD" (p. 142). That he is a bit premature can be
seen in the letter Lee then gets from his friend at Harvard. "Your
charming letter and your equally charming credentials are here.
Your *vita* we have passed from hand to hand. A more relaxed, gay,
and informal presentation we have not seen in a long time. We are
in the process of revising it along more suitable lines. . ." (p. 143).
He goes on to say he is fairly confident that an offer will follow, and
it is arranged that Lee and representatives from Harvard will meet
in New York when Lee gets there.

Harold can only reply, "You are far from our best scholar (you are
no scholar at all). . . . [At Harvard] you would be most unhappy
with your shoelaces dragging" (pp. 170 - 71).

C. Sexual Freedom

Searle suggests that the only alternative to being a member of the
Dollar A Word Club is "to be a member of the Beat Generation" (p.
87). That actually is another option which is presenting itself to Lee.
It comes in the person of his friend from the old days, Whizzer
Harlow, who is living down in Santa Fe in a cabin with an Indian
woman. Whizzer writes to Lee from time to time to borrow money
and to moan maudlinly about Lee's "luck" in finishing all his
writing projects.

Whizzer has had many possibilities to support himself writing.
He has had endless women in endless cabins "on every continent
but Australia" (p. 39), but, a boxer like Lee, he has usually ended
by copping out on his writing projects, beating up everyone around
him, and taking off.

Lee sends him money, arranges for him to get a sort of grant to support himself, and sternly enjoins him to get back to his writing, among other things, in order to pay his back child-support.

Nevertheless there is something in Whizzer's life, its freedom from social or familial pressure and from the pressure of work, that attracts Lee. He himself hints broadly to his friends and even to his wife, Beth, that he is carrying on a stormy on-again-off-again affair with Cecile, "a lovely big girl" in the English department. And in the back of his mind—we never know how serious he is about this—is the plan, once he gets to New York, to have an affair with his old friend, the glamorous Shoshone actress Gabriella Bodeen.

This, as he begins to hint about his plans, is more and more distressing to his friends. He has a good wife and good children, seven of them in fact. As his friend Harold Rosenblatt writes, it is "not because we very much care who screws whom, but because we know how all that you and Beth have had and have done and have and are doing together has always been so binding right" (p. 172). Even Gabriella, in a charming letter listing all the things they will do together in New York, hopes, in the end, they won't "wrestle in elevators" (p. 165).

D. Physical Expression

Something else from Lee's past is drawing him. He had started out to be a more than competent heavyweight boxer. Now suddenly Garafolo, his old fight manager, writes to tell him about a very fine new heavyweight he has. They are having a hard time getting started, and he wants Lee to invest some money in him. The proposition is irresistible to Lee. Irwin, the new fighter, is just the kind of man Lee would like to relate to. He thinks and lives fighting every minute. He, literally, has to punch the bag a little every day, as Lee writes a little every day. And best of all, he is having a hard time because he is a fighter's fighter; and in these corrupt, commercialized days only the flashy television fighter is making it, the fighter whose gross movements "explain" themselves to the ignorant television audience. Irwin's best hit is his deceptively punishing left hand, which can hardly even be noticed on television.

But Lee's motives in investing in him are not entirely disinterested. He wants to take an active interest in managing Irwin and perhaps vicariously live the career he might have had. He begins by arguing with Garafolo that Irwin can be hit over his left hand. Garafolo—and this is a trait he shares with Lee's wife and truest friends—will not flatter Lee, even though, at this moment, he needs money from him. "I will be glad to see you here [at the training camp], but I expeck you to keep your mouth shut except when eating and me do all the handling of Irwin necessary" (p. 162). Lee thinks he knows better and goes to the camp specifically to instruct Irwin. Unwittingly, he has put himself in the position of Enright and his "play doctor"—of the man who, because he has money invested, thinks he knows as much as the man who works daily in his trade. At the end of a towering argument he finally blurts out: " 'You know who can hit you over the jab?' I said to Irwin. 'Me.' " Irwin, whose trade is not the use of words, only replies, " 'When?' "

"He is not any bigger than I am, nor, fundamentally, in any better condition. I was handsome in orange tights." Lee forgets that he himself, however, has not been punching a bag every day. A moment later "he hit me with his right hand, and I was further defined" (p. 226).

IV *Definition*

In the background is the fact that Lee is up for tenure in his department. However much he may joke about the matter, the suspense is having its effect on his actions. While the official body sits in judgment on his professional life, his creative endeavor, and his personal character, he cannot stop himself from doing the same. The truth is, he begins to panic. He writes jokingly to his friend Harold, "Madly shall I cultivate my Tenure. Madly shall I assume administrative responsibilities" (p. 6). But instead of becoming sycophantic, with characteristic if misguided integrity, he turns almost wantonly against those of his true friends who are on the tenure committee and who would be supporting him. First he plays an inconsiderate, totally pointless prank on old Mr. Outerbridge, a wise and kindly senior member of the faculty, on the point of retirement after a distinguished career. Next, when Paul Purdy, chairman of the committee, appoints Cecile to it, Lee, to keep up the pretense none of them had believed anyway that he had just broken off a torrid affair with her, in a simulated rage at this "betrayal" by Paul, takes back his play from him. Then, to cap this childish behavior, he shows his wife a letter from Harold which discusses his possible involvement with Cecile.

It is as if, faced with the prospect of coming to terms with his life,
he is on the point of quitting everything, like his buddy Whizzer,
beating up everyone around him, and running off. At the beginning
of the novel he had jocularly projected the action into the future in
order to look back on his completed life: "It will be seen that,
although I was surely a fool, I had desirable friends and nasty
enemies" (p. 7). Just as with Henry Wiggen in *The Southpaw*, it is
in fact his good friends, refusing to humor him and seeing through
to what is fundamentally decent in him, who save him—by reminding him of what *is* good in him.

First comes a wonderful, kindly letter from Mr. Outerbridge,
who, far from being offended, has seen immediately to the bottom
of Lee's actions, a case of the "jitters" (pp. 116 - 17). He gently
builds Lee up, reminding him of his many extraordinary virtues,
and points out to him the pleasures and advantages of the profession of teaching. Lee, who had been taking the line that he was too
good to be a teacher, perhaps at this juncture needed reassurance
that he was indeed good *enough* to be a teacher. What he had
stupidly and unforgivably done to his friend Paul he at least partially undoes by immediately sending back the play and getting Harold
to phone Paul from Yale to try to patch things up. His wife also
knows him too well to believe in his pretended affairs. It is Harold,
his closest friend, who takes him most sternly to task, telling him
what a will-o'-the-wisp his 12 ½ % investment in a fighter is, how
miserable he would be at Harvard, how idiotic he is to take the play
away from Paul, who loves it and understands it as well as he does;
and as for his pretended affairs, they are "only a hangover from
boyhood days in Utah, where manhood was measured in that misguided way. We have always thought you man enough, except in-
sofar as you felt the need to 'prove' it" (p. 173). Harold has already
explained:

I have not for a moment believed that you are seriously worried about
your tenure. . . . Idle, you sought conflict. . . . But you err to seek it
within the minds of your colleagues: your enemies are very few. You are far
from our best scholar (you are no scholar at all) and you may not be our
most perfect teacher, but you, whose door, whose cabinets are always open,
whose correspondence lies scattered about, whose keys are always in their
locks (unless they be outside in your ignition), you who in your limitless
confidence own no briefcase, carry no notes, nor wear the honor pins nor
the titular badges of your profession—tell me who can dare to vote against
your openness? What combination of five or three can possibly be found to
deny your value? (pp. 169 - 70).

Like the others, Harold offers Lee generous praise of his good traits, frank criticism of his bad. Enright, the producer, and the other hacks were surrounded by yes-men who praised them in exchange for money. Lee is surrounded by true friends who guide him to the definition of himself he is seeking. "I am hoping," Harold writes, "this letter will reach you before you steam off on your vague mission to New York. Stay where you are" (p. 169).

Ironically, while all this good advice is still failing to get through to Lee, he is himself, in his true role of teacher and friend, giving similar advice to others. At one point, as a member of the personnel committee, we see him writing a very Outerbridgian letter to a new young faculty member, praising and encouraging him and pointing out the satisfactions possible to him in his chosen profession. At other points, we see him writing paternal letters to Whizzer, advising him to stay put and do his writing and remember his responsibilities. "Every man, if he be a man, barters a part of his freedom so that the world of children might survive" (p. 80). Most of all he enjoins him not to come to New York with him—as Whizzer has spontaneously decided to drop everything and do.

"Wake up, stupid!" his tenure committee observes he sometimes shouts to obstinately impenetrable students. The words are perhaps ringing in his ears when Garafolo "sat me up with the salts to my nose, and he said, 'Lee, every man to their own trade' " (p. 226). Lee had long before this, in a letter to his brother in Utah, written, "I am a natural story-teller . . . just as Alexander Irwin is a natural boxer, just as you are a natural farmer, and every good man plays his role, and no role is more important than any other role, and nobody is better than anybody else" (p. 110 - 11). At last he has come to accept it himself. He walks out on the producer and his play doctor, stands up the Harvard delegation, and heads for home, leaving Whizzer,—who has just shown up in New York, to go on acting out what is most infantile in Lee's own dreams—one day about to marry Gabriella Bodeen, the next proposing to someone else.

If we had any doubts about the quality of his relationship with his wife, these are dispelled toward the end when we see that in New York, away from home, all his longest, truest letters are to Beth. "Certainly I do not belong on Broadway," he writes her, "nor in the prize ring. Neither a Utah farm nor Harvard suits my taste. I am in sympathy with neither the beat generation nor The Dollar A Word Club. Tom Katt [the pilot] is dead, and Whizzer Harlow I have outgrown. I am the product of the process of elimination: my choice seems to be made for me. It is the reality. Why buck history?" (p. 227).

The tenure committee meets for one minute before unanimously granting him tenure.

V   Wake Up, Stupid *as Eighteenth-Century Novel*

In chapter three I suggested ways in which *The Southpaw* resembled the eighteenth-century classic *Tom Jones. Wake Up, Stupid* is even more closely and directly connected with the eighteenth century. Obviously, the epistolary structure is immediately reminiscent of the novels of Samuel Richardson, inventor of the form. But other allusions to the period abound: the play Lee has just completed at the outset of the novel is called *Boswell's Manhattan Journal.* Throughout the book Lee is reading Boswell's *Life of Johnson,* and his Harvard friends refer to his reputation for Boswell scholarship. His friend Harold Rosenblatt is, during the course of the novel, at Yale studying the Yale collection of Boswell papers. A dog which is a character in one of Lee's novels is named Lord Chesterfield. Other characters in *Wake Up, Stupid* include his friend Whizzer Harolow (an echo of Richardson's Clarissa Harlowe) and a new instructor, W. Wycherley Wood (named for a prominent Restoration dramatist). A poet colleague of Lee's is named Clinch, a standard tag-name in Restoration and eighteenth-century drama for a poet. The turning of the various hack writers into illiterate buffoons is typical of eighteenth-century burlesques of "grub street."

But the connection with the eighteenth-century is more than merely structural or textural. For the theme itself is typical of the Age of Reason and Neo-classical restraint, as expressed, for instance, by Imlac in Samuel Johnson's *Rasselas:* "It is our business to consider what beings like us may perform; each laboring for his own happiness, by promoting within his circle, however narrow, the happiness of others."

VI   *The Anarchic Gesture*

But living with reason is more restricting than living with dreams, just as mortality is necessarily briefer and more confining than immortality. Harris's characters do not achieve maturity without struggle; and at the last instant before acceptance, before definition, there often occurs in his novels an anarchic gesture. We see it in a small way when Henry Wiggen turns about on the mound and addresses the massed stadium and peering television cameras with "the old sign—1 finger up," sort of the *ur* gesture with which man defies his fate. Jacob, at the moment of total absurdity, with all that he had been taught and firmly believed at last proven false, turns and walks away from the army—his official connection with a depraved society—and goes AWOL. Lee, all his childish dreams remorselessly shown to him for what they are, steals a car in New York and ends up in a jail cell in Chicago.

There is something inescapably conservative in the movement of a novel from immaturity to maturity, for maturity can only imply a coming to terms with oneself and the world one must live in, a shift from rebellion to reconciliation, a "bartering" of part of one's freedom, a cessation from "bucking" history, a giving up of "the role of romantic lover" to become "solid citizen" (p. 222). Although maturity may express itself socially it is in fact deeply personal. It involves an acceptance of personal limitation and personal mortality, but with these an obligation to devote one's life to whatever is best in oneself. To arrive at a true estimate of himself, Henry Wiggen had to see through the seductions of headlines, money, glamorous women; Jacob Epstein had to discover that his real duty was not to love the world but to love individuals, that true patriotism was in opposing war and accepting love instead; Lee has to discover his theme: "You know, I think that's what my play is about—work, work, involve yourself in the life outside yourself, and the life inside yourself will unite with the life outside yourself, and *there* will be your art" (p. 210).

What shows man's wisdom is his accepting and making the most of the role fate has given him; what shows his humanity is that one last anarchic gesture.

VII   The Goy

I suggested at the beginning of this chapter that *Wake Up, Stupid* and *The Goy* are two versions of the same story. This is not immediately evident in reading *The Goy*. Harris's novels typically are pellucid and bright; this one is dark and murky. Typically, action and character are directly expressive of theme: search beneath the surface and we find that surface extended and enriched—but unchanged. In this novel, however, there is scarcely any action at all; characters fuse or trade roles, and almost all is internal, under the surface.

What action there is can be told quickly: Westrum, the goy of the title, is a renowned historian, writer of the famous *A History of the Past World*. Although he has a Jewish wife, a Jewish mistress, half-Jewish sons, he is tall, blond, straight-nosed, speaks with a midwestern twang: he is distrusted by Jews at sight, and he feels that he is being exiled from New York ("City of Jews") and his university position there by them. As the novel opens he is driving with his wife and youngest son, Terence, to the Midwest, to the prestigious Center, where he may be offered a seat to pursue his scholarship—mainly, in this case, to continue his lifelong journal. The Seating Committee, all Jews, are suspicious of him, especially the head of the committee, Benstock. Westrum, to get a moral advantage over Benstock, presents himself as a model of purity. He does not smoke or drink before Benstock and confides to him that despite his fame and great personal attractiveness, he has never slept with any woman but his wife, and not with her until they were married.

In the meantime, while carrying on a correspondence with his mistress in New York, he begins working toward acquiring a new mistress at the Center, Harriet Weinberg, wife of one of the other members of the committee. He sends for Miss Sanantone, his secretary of the past ten years, and settles her in at the Center, so she can continue transcribing his daily shorthand notes into his journal, in which he records everything which transpires. He has always thought of her as "an attachment to his typewriter" (p. 76),[8] a neutral moral agent who could somehow type up everything about his private life and yet retain none of it in her head. Instead, we find, she has been avidly following the account of his activities like a wonderful flesh-and-blood movie. But she misses New York, and especially her boyfriend there, a "make-work" detective named Hawkes. Hawkes, for his part, suspects Westrum has taken Miss Sanantone out to the Midwest for immoral purposes. So they both begin working to get Westrum to come back to New York, bringing Miss Sanantone with him. As a first step, with Miss Sanantone's help, Hawkes finds out the identity of Westrum's mistress—the wife of one of the trustees of the university in New York. But in the meantime, at Hawkes's request, Miss Sanantone has carefully deleted some unflattering references to him in the journal. Westrum discovers this alteration to the sacred text and instantly fires her.

By this time, with his guise of purity, Westrum has finally won the confidence of Benstock and the Seating Committee. They will give him a seat for as long as he wants and purchase his journal.

Overjoyed at this chance to start a new life, for once accepted rather than rejected, a brand-new mistress in prospect, he returns to New York to clear up his business there. The first thing he does is visit his old mistress, but they are confronted in their trysting place by Hawkes, who tells him that he must return to New York for good and rehire Miss Sanantone, or the news of his mistress will become very public.

Westrum realizes he has no choice and gives in. His mistress, of course, is secretly delighted to have him back. The university, which Westrum only imagined was exiling him, takes him back with open arms—it had only been waiting for a commitment from him that he would stay. And Westrum himself realizes he is back where he belongs.

VIII   The Goy *and* Wake Up, Stupid

The Goy, with its dark tone and its extreme actions, is so untypical of Harris's work that it comes almost as a surprise to find how characteristic its ingredients are, how much the novel echoes, in fact, though from the shadow side, a work so typical of Harris as *Wake Up, Stupid.* To begin with, it retains from the preceding novel at least a vestige of the Neo-classical period: Westrum's journal, like Pepys's *Diary*—and the parallel is intended—is written in a private shorthand, in which he frankly includes every detail from his public and private life. When Pepys was writing about his mistress, he used a further concealment, not only writing in shorthand but in French as well. The only reticence in Westrum's journal is that he never mentions his mistress by name, always referring to her as "Madame."

Once more, as in *Wake Up, Stupid,* we have as protagonist an athlete-intellectual. Westrum, prestigious scholar and author, former member of a presidential commission on population, though fifty years old, is still tall and blond, youthful and fit. "It was easy to see the hero's attraction for women, how trim how slim, how lithe he was, how open his smile, how even his teeth" (p. 227). In summer he daily swam a thousand yards in nineteen minutes; in fall, as temperatures cooled, he changed to running, doing a daily two miles in thirteen minutes thirty seconds. In the cold weather he cycled each day, eight miles in seventeen minutes fifty seconds. In bed he was "superb," well able to take care of his wife and mistress and look around for more besides.

In this last matter—and here is part of Harris's shift to more ex-

treme statement—unlike Henry Wiggen and Lee Youngdahl, he
carries out his infidelities rather than merely hungering after them.

Again like Lee Youngdahl (and Harris himself), Westrum is a
compulsive writer. He has passed the fifty-thousandth page of his
daily journal, filling those around him with admiration and dismay.
As Miss Sanantone bemusedly expressed it, "Did you ever hear of a
man who spent half his life writing down the other half?" (p. 87).
But Westrum (who thought of himself as "living his life twice to understand it once"—p. 57) claimed writing the journal was not
"stopping his life, it *was* his life, it was a thing he'd made" (p. 114).
We recall Harris's own similar statement: "For a writer who has advanced beyond a certain stage of his life, the work itself is experience."

IX   The Autobiographical Impulse

The autobiographical impulse has here the same thematic
justification as in other of Harris's writings, for Westrum's theory of
history is Harris's theory of fiction: namely that the best way to tell
the history of Everyman is to examine in painstaking detail the life
of any man, and that the man the author knows best and in most
detail is himself. Westrum thinks of himself as one "for whom
history was accessible only by a study of persons, of individual men
and women consumed by private goals and passions, seeking glory
in their own time by humiliation of particular enemies, not by a
study of reigning theories of existence but by the study of lovers and
mistresses, wives and fathers and children" (p. 206). (Pepys's intimate diary, it is appropriate to mention here, remains the single
most important source of information on Restoration London).

Having completed his great *History of the Past World*, Westrum
"had discovered to his chagrin that he had written less a history of
the world than an account of his own mind, carved from his Journal" (p. 9): As he sees it,

The principal value of the work had been its freeing him into a
knowledge of himself as he had been. With the fame of the book . . .
Westrum became new beyond the Westrum he had been, oddly celebrated,
whose reward was his release from anonymity or material care into freedom
and vast confidence to proceed knowingly and consciously now upon lines
established by accident. . . . Having revealed so much of the world in the
disguise of historian, he believed he could now reveal even more as
Westrum himself, throwing off all disguise, with a craft greater and deeper

now because more conscious . . . prepared by training and by inclination to display for the mind of history his own true mind and passion heretofore concealed, the worst or most violent or secret parts of himself, along with the noblest. He would prepare his Journal for the eye of the public world, if not in his own generation then afterward. Thereby he would perform the single service within his power (p. 20).[9]

Benstock, thinking of purchasing the journal for the Center, "saw that the Journal might be, by seeing one man so close in infinite detail, a portrait of many men themselves revealed by symbol, clarified, renewed, refreshed, made well, relieved to discover themselves not uniquely troubled but eternally natural children of creation" (p. 83). There is, then, a therapeutic, Freudian motive to it, the liberating knowledge that the evil in our own soul is likewise in every soul, is part of the good and bad in the makeup of normal and even excellent men, so that no one is singularly depraved.

The communication of this perception is, perhaps, a key to the novel and to its tone. For, rather than an autobiography, it is no less than an extended autopsychoanalysis that we are presented with. Like Youngdahl, Westrum, during the course of the novel, is being defined. As the tenure committee sat in judgment of Lee, so the Seating Committee at the Center is judging Westrum, and this knowledge that he is being scrutinized has precipitated in him an urgent need to scrutinize himself. Youngdahl had felt life, "history," trapping him into a mode of existence too meager for his capacity. Westrum is likewise prisoner, but in this case he is his own jailer, keeping himself, with his rigid discipline, in powerful check, for fear of what his real nature might be. He ran or swam or cycled "to subdue the heat of his hatreds, and to ease or silence the dialogue between himself and imagined enemies. The more strenuous his exercise the less the violence of his antagonisms. In his heart lay murder" (p. 12). Lee in *Wake Up, Stupid* quested after himself in broad daylight, more or less charmingly acting out his desires. There was the possibility of danger, but in the end nothing was really done, no one was hurt, at least not permanently. It is different with Westrum, whose potential to strike out against his own friends is all too real, who must battle himself deep in the darkness of his own unconscious.

Lee, panicking, imagining his tenure in doubt, had snatched his play away from his friend Paul Purdy, an action quickly rectified. Westrum's action was not so innocent. Imagining himself exiled, in a moment of unreasoning fury he had struck his son with his hand,

and broken his back, leaving him partially crippled for the rest of his life.

X   The Dark Man

As an epigraph to the novel, Harris quotes part of a letter sent to him by an astrologer: "Do you realize that you are also symbolically coming to terms with the Dark Man in your own depths? What you are doing outwardly is enacting a sort of inner drama in symbolic form. I dislike people who are averse to the dark races, not merely for humanitarian reasons, but because those who deny the dark are instinct suppressors and life deniers." To an unusual degree the epigraph gives, in capsule form, both the action and resolution of the novel.

At the beginning of the novel Westrum, with his wife and son, are driving from New York to "the Center." It is located twelve hundred miles due west, which is to say that, among other things, the Center is also geographically approximately in the center of the county. And Westrum, as representative American (as his name and role in the novel indicate him to be), is symbolically returning to the center of himself, returning—in the best tradition of psychoanalysis—to the seat of his childhood fixation; for it turns out that he was born and raised within a few miles of the Center, in the town of Brest. "Brest" is almost too good a name for the source that one returns to, but it has another signification as well. The towns located around the Center are Brest, Paree, and New Hamburg, three cities which, taken together, describe a line through the extent of Western Europe, so that we find encapsulated in the heart of innocent America its corrupt Old-World origins, and Westrum is delving into his racial memory as well. In due course, Westrum will go all the way back home and try to come to terms with his fascist father, but he puts off this journey repeatedly. He wants to get himself in order first. He begins, thus close to home, living at the Center, to try to reestablish his life.

His life here quickly almost exactly duplicates his life in New York. Benstock, chairman of the Seating Committee, is practically interchangeable with Tikvah, his brother-in-law, who is vice-chancellor of the university in New York. Harriet Weinberg, wife of another member of the committee, is a beautiful dark Jewess like his mistress in New York, who is wife of a trustee of the university. He begins making plans to make her his mistress here. He already has with him his wife and son and soon sends for his secretary, getting her back to work on the daily task of transcribing, indexing, and filing away his journal as, day by day, he adds to it.

The journal, the vast, comprehensive record of every thought, feeling, and encounter he has had over the years, the infallible corrective for his fallible memory, is in many respects like that other comprehensive repository, the unconscious, and it is in this way he uses it, sifting and searching it, looking for the source of that moment of violence in that "most terrible night of their lives" (p. 10). Had he shouted, in the act of striking, "You little Jew!" or words to that effect? Was he, in his inmost heart, fight it as he may, a fascist anti-Semite like his father?

The first clue he gets comes from another doppelgänger. Harriet's husband, Harvey Weinberg—inept, graceless, perspiring, a physical wreck—reminds him of someone from his deep past. He deliberately uses his unconscious to find out who the person is, putting the whole question out of his mind, then having it suddenly come floating up to him in the moment before falling asleep. He remembers, to begin with, only a fragment of the incident: "At that moment he saw clearly the face of the principal at Brest whom his father had driven from the school and from the town, and he saw the face of a schoolmate, too. It was a boy. And he saw the circumstances, too, himself, his father, the principal, the boy, clear faces in a distant clouded circumstance" (p. 60). Later, through free association, he picks up the boy's name, Turtleman. Then he can look him up in the journal, and, forced by necessity visit his mother and father and get more information from them. Then finally, revisiting the school where the incident took place, he at last can get the whole story together. At first he only sees the boy lying at his feet, and hears his friends cheering him on for giving it to the little Jew. The principal insists that he apologize to Turtleman, he refuses, and his father has the principal run out of town.

Ultimately the whole story comes clear: the boy had been climbing up on a window ledge, but very clumsily. Westrum had sought to help this boy, who was usually derided and trampled on by the other students. In sheer amazement and gratitude, the boy lost his grip and fell. The principal, misunderstanding the event, asked Westrum to apologize, which of course he refused to do, not having done anything.

His father had finally driven the Turtlemans (and every other Jewish family as well) out of the town. The Turtlemans had hated

Westrum, assuming he was the same as his father, but luckily Westrum had met Turtleman just as Turtleman was going overseas to war and had explained himself, dissociating himself from his father, and they had parted friends.

This much of Westrum's past was reassuring, and perhaps gave him the courage to go on to the main issue, the reason behind his violence to his own son. But he used a different psychoanalytical technique for working out this problem, the clinical technique of "abreaction," or acting out the compulsive situation, to analyze it and get control of it.

His neurosis began with his fear of being "exiled" by the Jews. He had headed the President's Population Inquiry until Justice Lerman (who is actually his mistress's husband) tells him he will no longer be needed, exiling him, Westrum feels, from Washington. As the novel opens, he is leaving New York, believing that Tikvah is exiling him from the university. His very first words in the novel—addressing his wife—are "Your brother has driven me into exile." He is now in some fear that Benstock will drive him from the Center, again into exile.

It is easy to see that this fear has come to him from his father. Nearly the first words the father addresses to Westrum, when the son visits, are, "They drove you out of Washington, too, did they, and now out of New York as well. The knives are out for the likes of you, you know. They'll rip you up, those professors will" (p. 168). And finally, "They'll drive you out of that joint, too" (p. 170), referring to the Center. To his father, who sees things in simple terms, it is purely a matter of nature. "It's natural, and I am a natural man. It's in my nature to close myself off from the people I'm not, and I respect them more when they close themselves off from me, too. I don't go where I'm not wanted" (p. 176).

But Westrum knows it is not so simple, that his father, in the name of nature, made Jews the scapegoat for all that was evil within himself.

It was not until after Lerman fired him, exiled him from Washington, that, on some small pretext (Terence had dropped and broken a fruit bowl), he struck out and maimed his son. Had he shouted *Jew*? Leaving New York in exile, or "imagined exile" (p. 3), he is once more cool, restrained, outwardly calm, but his wife recognizes the dangerous mood, and she and Terence tiptoe around him.

It is not until later, under the influence of his suspicion that

Benstock is going to refuse him a seat at the Center, that Westrum finds himself again in a situation identical to that of the night he struck Terence. Although his wife has tried to stop the scene, he deliberately allows it to proceed. He is having an argument with his son, who, defying him, has thrown a fireplace bellows on the floor:

> "Pick up the bellows," his father said.
> "First I'll button the shirt," said Terence.
> "First you'll pick up the bellows," Westrum said. His voice was low, and he knew that no voice would move Terence, and he knew, too, now at last, the nature of the moment: that his rage had arisen then and now not because of a bowl or bellows upon the floor but because the moment was the moment of exile—exiled then by Lerman from Washington, exiled now by Benstock from the Center. It was all quite clear and simple. A man required only fifty thousand pages of Journal closely studied to explain himself to himself. . . .
> "All right," said Westrum, "button your shirt first" (pp. 218 - 19).

He had taken a chance by allowing the fateful situation to re-create itself, but this time, bringing more knowledge and wisdom to it, he was able to observe and learn more about his fury and thereby control it.

The final cathartic scene comes, not with Terence, but with his mistress, when they are trapped by the detective Hawkes. He has, after all, been accepted at the Center, and now Hawkes has exiled him from it. The moment Hawkes leaves him alone with his mistress, they find themselves in a fight over some trivial thing, and he strikes her.

> "Turn it loose," he said, whose voice so moderated suggested hardly more than the disappointment of a morning gone bad, but whose eyes, his mistress saw, were distant with rage, but saw too late, arms wide, dancing on her toes toward him, her motion beyond recall. It was not she he struck, but someone else in another moment in another place, with studious deliberation, as if he were both assailant and witness, and his mind listened to himself and heard himself cry, "Turn it loose I said," not *Jew* or *little Jew* but only *Turn it loose I said*, and she fell. "You see," he said, "you see, I never called him that," and he knelt beside her.
> "I see," she said (she'd see with only one eye for a while)" (p. 267).

His main fear, that his father has left him in his American heart an anti-Semite, has apparently been groundless. There may be a number of other bad things in his character, but not this particular evil, and secure in himself now he may be able to stop probing and testing all Jews he comes into contact with, almost forcing them to reject him, for the sake of finding out how he will respond.

XI   *Ice-water Westrum*

"Ice-water Westrum" had been his nickname when he was a celebrity in Washington, chairing the President's Population Inquiry. He gained the nickname partly for his coolness and absolute discipline, but also because at social functions he was known only to drink ice water. This last was a pose, for he drank intoxicating beverages with his mistress and with his wife, but in public he preserved his purity. The posture gave him more leverage. He had, for instance, told his brother-in-law Tikvah, just as he later tells Benstock, that he had never slept with any woman but his wife, which "elevated him in Tikvah's mind to a plane of moral sturdiness which accounted for everything else. Not Westrum's accidental blessing but Westrum's moral striving was the secret of his success" (p. 4). As he tells Benstock he does not smoke or drink: "*Good,* he thought, *overwhelm him with moral accomplishment,* he'd play the part of austerity here, he'd be old settler, old upright self-denying American, cling to old virtues for the eyes of new Jews, who'd give him all the Seat he wanted out of their own scrupulous love of justice" (pp. 28 - 29). At one point later in the novel, a desperate and miserable Benstock asks Westrum to accompany him to a little bar he knew:

Why not why not? thought Westrum, for he loved noisy little bars and big girls and little girls singing and stripping . . . why not go instead with Benstock, who needed him now . . . why not relieve Benstock this night of the burden of Westrum, come clean with Benstock, do a kindness, show Benstock that he, too, Westrum, was only a man like any other, nothing superior about him at all, hungry for a broiled steak, nor above a whiskey, either? Such moments as these he had had with Tikvah, too, but never been able to abandon the person he had become (p. 189).

Part, indeed, of Westrum's problem is his inability to let himself go:

In the beginning he had learned all he knew of the world from printed pages. He knew no other way of talking back or telling out. From his own detestable father he had learned very little, and that all wrong, where coldness and silence were the code of the house. Thus, when the time came, and he fell among the Jews, he rejoiced, he admired them to extravagance, he envied them their talk, their frankness, their uncensored passion, the unfenced limits of their debate, partaking without repaying in kind, sitting silent and seeming cold, not because he chose that way but because he was incapable of passion except upon paper.

And he married into them as soon as he could (p. 42).

"The trouble with my fascist father," he says, "is that he never let himself go" (p. 181). It is of course Westrum's own fear of being a fascist which holds him back. What would he find if he let himself *be* himself? It is most important to him to trace back the affair with Turtleman and especially to know what he said at that moment of release when he struck his son, because if he had called the boy *Jew*, he would be repeating that old reflex of his father's of blaming misfortunes of any kind on a simplified, externally projected enemy, the Jews.

XII *Definition*

As he analyzes himself and begins to find reassuring evidence that he is not after all his father's son, he begins trying to loosen up. He sees Benstock and his son kissing unashamedly on the lips, with warmth and affection, and he yearns to be more expressive with his own son, but it is a difficult response to teach himself. When his son wins a contest he has been working on throughout the course of the novel, Westrum goes so far as putting his hand on his shoulder. But before he can do more than that, Harvey Weinberg runs up and embraces Westrum and Terence both. One last experience is necessary before Westrum can relax completely.

Ironically, this experience, which once and for all defines him, is to be *truly* exiled for the first time in the novel. For we have learned, reading between the lines, that the other exiles were (perhaps unconsciously) brought on by Westrum himself. He had lost the Washington job because he made it known that everything he did was going down in his journal, which would one day be published, and much that was going on may have been sensitive or at least embarrassing to the powers he was working for. He had brought about his own exile from the university by demanding of his brother-in-law a salary obviously higher than the school could afford. At the Center he had demanded an outrageous price for his journal—sight unseen.

The true exile comes at the hands of Hawkes, his threat of

blackmail forcing Westrum to leave the Center. What is significant is that, far from being a Jew, Hawkes is a Jew hater, a fascist anti-Semite himself, and, for all the delightful energy with which Hawkes and Miss Sanantone have been presented to us as characters, they are obviously much lesser people than Westrum, people whose humanity Westrum had scarcely deigned to notice, Miss Sanantone being to him an attachment to his typewriter and Hawkes coming into his consciousness only as a "make-work" detective whose name he could never remember, Miss Sanantone's "friend."

Accepted by the Center, he had meant to go back and settle in his home town, work in his father's attic as he had as a child, free now from all his fears about himself. And at this very moment he finds himself driven from his town by an anti-Semite, just as the original families of Jews had been driven from the town by his father. He finds himself not exiled *from* New York by the Jews, but *to* New York by the fascists.

He is amazed at how glad he is to return to the city. He spontaneously kisses Tikvah's wife, embraces Tikvah, and "at last himself became a Jew today, he felt, exiled forever from Brest to the place of his true belonging, city of Jews" (p. 268).

XIII   *The Problems with* The Goy

I have tried to suggest that the novel has a structure, a theme, a control—yet, all that said, it is not an entirely satisfactory book. Where it is strongest is in those places that Harris is always strong, in the lively presentation of character and in the tense or comic dialogue between characters at moments of confrontation. The most beautifully rendered characters in the book are mainly those who might be called the "low-life" characters, the vigorous, sharp, and bitter old fascist father, the chain-smoking Miss Sanantone, her boyfriend Hawkes, with his Dick Tracy - like features, and the black holes in his teeth, and Westrum's fine, stubborn, convincingly adolescent son Terence, with his ever handy movie camera, "historian upon film, as his father was historian on paper" (p. 200). Whenever any of these are on stage, the action quickens marvelously. Especially fine is the scene where the family goes to visit Westrum's father or the one where Westrum accuses Miss Sanantone of altering the journal, or almost any scene with Terence in it. But these scenes are all too few, and all too often we are confronting the rather lookalike Jews, imported, one sometimes feels, from some other novel rather than from life. And usually we are deep in Westrum's mind. Westrum fluctuates. He is and is not a good character—his internal life is more convincing than his external behavior. Harris does not always seem to be certain how he wants to handle him. The rather stern and analytic person of his inner lucubrations is convincing enough, interesting enough, but Harris keeps trying to add on to him, from the outside, moments of gaiety, or sudden sympathy, or devil-may-care prankishness, which do not seem to fit him. At times Westrum lapses into a sort of smug and callow *machismo* that is only embarrassing. Girls he picks up hitchhiking are "grateful," and indeed "he reckoned now, by the devices of his memory assisted by his Journal, that he belonged to that company of men more active than numerous who had had at least one lady, fine or otherwise, young or otherwise, in most of the states of the union" (p. 4) and when he meets his mistress they customarily fall upon one another "giving and receiving every pleasure their imaginations could devise" (p. 256). We suspect the words are meant as a delightful liberation for us all.

Except that she is necessary for certain sorts of thematic statement, one wonders why Harris has Westrum *have* a mistress. There is nothing the matter with Westrum's wife, who is an equally dark, beautiful Jewess, only perhaps a bit more intelligent than the mistress, and certainly with less of what D. H. Lawrence would call "sex on the head." Is it just that Harris felt he had perhaps pulled too many punches in *Wake Up, Stupid?* All is charm and lightness in that book; the chances for ugliness are there, but are pulled back from. Here all is actualized, and there is a certain amount of genuine cruelty, as in the portrayal of that "shaking wreck" Henry Weinberg. In this respect *The Goy* is indeed a braver book, but not really more honest, because Harris, having portrayed cruelty to friends, infidelity, irremediable harm, finally does try to pull back and convince us that just as in *Wake Up, Stupid*, all will end up charming, forgiveable, remediable.

In fairness, we must observe that what Harris has tried to do is difficult. He has attempted, while preserving our sympathy for his character, to have that character act out symbolically all the dreck that—as we know in this post-Freudian age—is present in the souls of every one of us. But we still tend to judge people, if not by their desires, then by whether they act on them or not. Self-realization is a noble goal, but not if it can only be achieved at the expense of others. That after all was one of the morals of *Wake Up, Stupid* and intermittently of this book too.

Harris, it appears to me, started out to make *The Goy* a much tougher book, but then he kept hedging his bet, and the result was a book perhaps a bit uncertain in intention.

Nevertheless, the attempt to write such a difficult book was valuable for him. He ended by learning the solutions to the problems he struggled not altogether successfully with here. The result was the very considerable success of the novel to follow.

CHAPTER 6

The New Synthesis:
Killing Everybody

H ARRIS is unusual among American writers, whose general
pattern is to write a few brilliant books at the beginning of
their careers; and then, locked into the form of some past achievement, to write successively weaker imitations of them. Harris once
remarked that "there are at least a dozen writers now dashing about
the United States whose significant work was long ago done, their
fame made and their money spent, whose gracelessness depresses us
all."[1] He himself has been writing with great consistency of purpose
and yet with continual invention and exploration, for something like
thirty years. Since the time he learned, beginning his third novel,
"that what matters is how well you write, how truly, not what you
write about, not timeliness or topicality,"[2] he has been working with
essentially the same themes, which gives his work the sort of con-
tinuity the best European writers have; and yet he has not repeated,
because what he has addressed himself to over and over are the
solutions to the formal and technical problems of embodying his
themes, and he has done this with an almost total disregard for
fashions or criticism or popularity.

These themes and the means for embodying them in fictions, are,
of course, precisely what has involved us in the preceding chapters.
Let me recapitulate them: (1) the theme of any man as Everyman:
an almost medieval insistence on the representative quality of each
man, and particularly of the writer, who because of his self-
consciousness has the capacity to learn from experience, and in
writing about this experience to share it; (2) the major theme of the
learning process, particularly the learning of one's place in the
scheme of things, so that the processes of individuation and self-
definition determine most actions in the novels; (3) the antiwar
theme that war, as the great impersonal machinery for the destruc-

101

tion of young men, cuts off at the root any man's and thus Everyman's—the entire society's—opportunity to grow from experience; (4) an emerging theme that each man is a mixture of some good and much real bad and that growing is learning to distinguish one from the other, to control the worst and to act on the best—that the outcome, not the potential, determines whether man is worthy.

This last theme is particularly difficult to deal with in fiction. We may know well what lurks in our own unregenerate hearts and yet continue to regard ourselves highly. But we are less generous with characters in literature, who must be brave and honorable beyond our own courage and integrity if they are to gain even our tolerance. Harris began with Henry Wiggen, whose faults were many (some of them serious), but we forgave him because of his youth and lack of formal education and because in his own field, as a professional athlete, he excelled beyond our power to excel. Jacob Epstein's faults were negligible and readily excusable because of his extreme youth. With Lee Youngdahl, Harris makes his first sustained effort to present a flawed hero, a man who, under pressure, lashes out at those closest to him; but Harris deals with his conception gingerly. He first makes Lee a very charming person, remarkable in endowments, fortunate in friends, and then he never allows things to get too far out of hand. Not until *The Goy* does Harris face directly the problem of presenting a character filled with violence which he seeks in every way to control, but which nonetheless at times overpowers him, with irreparably harmful results. Even in this brave book, at the end Harris draws back a little, tries to tidy over some of the worst consequences. Still, we end up liking his hero less than we suspect Harris wants us to.

In his latest novel, *Killing Everybody*, Harris has realigned the elements of his past works into a new synthesis which brilliantly solves some past problems, despite the fact that this novel presents his most extreme statements so far, for its characters are filled with homicidal violence, sexual lust, and "perversions," and act freely on these, destroying, to the extent of their powers, the conventional framework of society. And yet, these are the "good" characters, those who win our sympathy and support. The book is an incredible achievement.

I   Killing Everybody

The action of the novel takes place within twenty-four hours. It begins with Brown, a headline-writer for the *Chronicle*, taking his dinner break and walking down to the campaign headquarters of McGinley, who is running for Congress. Brown's relationship with McGinley is complex. Twenty years before, another man, Stanley Krannick, had amused himself by torturing his own infant son. Brown, hearing of this, had sent Krannick a letter claiming to be from child welfare and saying an agent would be out the next morning to investigate him. Krannick had hastily left town, and Brown had moved in with Krannick's deserted wife, Luella, and has lived with her ever since, raising the boy, Junie, as his own son. Junie has imbibed Brown's pacifism and, on that account, has attempted to get a deferment from the draft. McGinley, at that time head of the draft board, has refused the deferment (although he was notorious for granting deferments in exchange for bribes), and Junie has gone off to Vietnam, where, refusing to carry a gun, he was soon killed.

Brown is outraged at McGinley's being alive when Junie is dead. Not only that, but McGinley (whose campaign slogan is "The West wasn't won with a registered gun") is almost certain to be elected to Congress in the next day's election. Desperate to take some action, Brown phones in a bomb threat, and the handshaking line in McGinley's headquarters is evacuated. McGinley, with no more campaigning to do, sneaks off for an illegal massage.

Luella runs a real-estate office which seems to do no business at all, despite the great amount of money she takes in every day. She is, despite her very nice figure, a prim, motherly woman. McGinley had once shaken her hand and told her how pretty she was, and now, to Brown's disgust, she wears a McGinley button, and has his name on the bumper sticker of her car. Brown puts it down to her supreme innocence.

The next morning we are introduced to another character, James Berberick, who sells classified ads at the *Chronicle*. His car, like Luella's, is covered with McGinley slogans. He had been sent to Vietnam also, but unlike Junie, he wanted to survive, so he had shot his way out, had killed men, women, children, perhaps even his own men—anyone, in short, who possibly came between him and his getting back home alive. His animal nature close to the surface, he is filled with a continual and ungovernable lust for women, which—when time does not allow him to make any more complicated arrangements—he slakes by means of quick trips to one of the city's many illegal massage parlors.

Suddenly we discover that Luella, who has successfully concealed the fact from the rather staid Brown, is actually the proprietress of a massage parlor (the real-estate office around the corner is just a front), patronized by both Berberick and McGinley. Now the plot emerges. Luella has convinced Berberick that for one who has killed so many, one more murder can scarcely matter. With the promise of a lifetime free pass plus some very special service, she has induced him to murder McGinley.

When McGinley comes for his appointment that night with Luella, he finds the front door of her establishment—which is down a narrow alley—locked. Disappointed, he steps back out into the alley, where Berberick is waiting. Berberick drives up behind him, gently knocks him down with the car, and shouting "Luella asked me to do this" (p. 261)[3] crushes him to death.

As the novel ends Luella is just introducing a horny and impecunious young policeman to the pleasures of her establishment and already beginning to hint to him that her former husband, Krannick, who had done considerable psychological harm to Junie which may have contributed to the boy's death, really does not deserve to live.

II *The Characters*

The real innovation, and perhaps even breakthrough, in this novel is in the deployment of characters. I have suggested that in past works Harris has used eighteenth-century models. Perhaps I can express the difference in this novel by saying that here Harris uses a nineteenth-century model—the model of, say, Thackeray in *Vanity Fair*. For this is, as the subtitle suggests Thackeray's work is, "A Novel Without a Hero." Harris began writing his mature novels with a semiliterate athlete hero, then he moved to an unathletic intellectual hero, and then combined these into an intellectual / athlete hero. Each of these types, effective in his particular role, led to certain kinds of developmental dead ends for Harris. The athlete finally had too small a vocabulary to say all that Harris knew to say, but on the other hand, Jacob, the four-eyed intellectual, though he could reason and judge, at last was limited in the actions—chiefly passive—that were possible to him. The athlete-intellectual would seem to have neither of these disadvantages, but turned out to have disadvantages of his own. Potent to act, and yet potent also to judge—and so to be judged—he was not only divided against himself, but risked dividing the reader against him too.

Killing Everybody has no central "hero." The characters are all ordinary people, a man who writes headlines for the *Chronicle*, another who sells classified ads for the same paper, a woman who runs a massage parlor, a young policeman, a young housewife, assorted husbands, wives, children, bosses—people who, for the most part, still live in the neighborhoods they grew up in, who know the people in the shops, nod to people on the street corners, are annoyed by their neighbor's barking dog. People we would scarcely glance at as they walked by us, and yet, as the omniscient author quickly shows us, people filled with the same inner flow of consciousness that we are, full of uncensored daydreams and fantasy and violence, motivated by odd and contradictory forces of trust and suspicion, benevolence and greed, lust and generosity; motivated often by outrage at an outer world whose institutions seem to express only our worst and never our best.

Because these characters are ordinary people, rather than paragons, we are less surprised (and disappointed) to find their minds so much like our own. Harris has confronted us with humanity—"any man" with a vengeance—and since we have not been asked especially to admire what we see, we end by not condemning these people. Rather, the opposite.

III   *Common Man, Innocent and Corrupt*

In the microworld of the novel, Brown and Luella, whom I will discuss in the next section, stand somewhat apart, but the rest of the characters represent ordinary humanity in its various guises. The treatment, as I have suggested above, is almost medieval, almost allegorical: the characters, for all their variety and complexity, have something simple and childlike about them, almost endlessly and momentarily capable of salvation or damnation, of innocence or corruption; and there is a profound—shall I call it Christian?—tolerance of each until he falls over that final precipice of absolute corruption when he makes of his fellow man an object, a possession—at which point he is summarily consigned to darkness.

The best characters have an Edenic—more, an animal—naturalness. "Smelly Jim" Berberick and Lala Ferne are the Adam and Eve of the novel. Both are corruptible through external machination, but savable in the same way, for both have an internal core of innocence, a "life force" with which they confront the "life deniers." Both, in their youth and inexperience, had been imposed on by evil forces, had become "possessions" of the bad characters. They had "hooked" another for the war: "It hadn't been like the advertisements. They'd advertised preparation for trades, skills, education, see the world, insurance benefits . . . but then once they hooked you they had you hooked: you forgot to read the small print, you were too young to know you should have read it . . . you were brutalized, and if you dared to desert all those indignities they stood you up and shot you. As for James, sensing how it was, he'd shot his way out of it" (p.183). Lala was married young to a man who considered her one more of his many possessions: "She had simply switched from her mother to Harold, doing whatever Harold said—buckled up her seatbelt, locked up all doors at all times, admitted no man to the house unless she knew who he was, washed out Louisa's mouth with soap when she said bad words within the hearing of neighbors and kept a careful track of every penny spent for whatever purpose like the goddam fool she was—first her mother's slave, now Harold's slave" (p. 83).

Their saving grace is their extreme horniness. Lala phones the *Chronicle* to take out a classified ad, and just the sound of Berberick's voice sends "ripples" through her body. Berberick, with his chronic "inability to resist" (p. 160), senses he has found a soul mate and comes to her house to take her ad in person. When he is excited, he sweats, and his powerful body odor had alienated his co-workers at the *Chronicle*, but Lala is turned on by it. In a minimum of time they have come together like animals in heat. Even more—Lala had compassionately brought into the house Christopher, a thirteen-year-old neglected child from the neighborhood, whose hard manly little body had also aroused her, and in a climactic scene she takes him from the front at the same moment Berberick takes her from the rear. "She was never so delighted" (p. 227).

Of such goings-on the prim Luella only comments "it was healthy, it was all of a piece with the will to live" (p. 197). Because the "good" characters' opposite numbers are the life-deniers. "They're trying to murder us," Berberick says, "because they don't love living enough. They're afraid of it. They can't enjoy themselves, so they kill people who do" (p. 222).

McGinley, for instance, head of the draft board, is running for Congress on the issue of not registering guns;[4] Stanley Krannick, Luella's husband, father of Junie, amused himself by holding his infant son's nostrils and mouth closed until he was nearly smothered; Christopher's parents lock him out all day while they are making money working overtime at the munitions factory, making bombs to drop on the Asian children; Harold, Lala's husband, who cares only about his many possessions, married Lala because she was fat, but lost interest in her when she slimmed down to normal size, because there was then less of her to own.

IV *The Legislator and the Executive*

Brown and Luella occupy a special place in the economy of the novel. Brown, we are told, "is the engine of our story" (p. 3). He has had his schooling at a religious seminary, Faith Calvary Central; and though he has fallen away from it, he has not lost what his foster son, Junie, had called a "sophisticated moral code" (p. 25). His hugely developed sense of the injustice of the world, the contrasts "between the mighty and the humble, the rich and the poor, the well and the ill, the living and the dead" (p. 128), particularly his dead Junie, keep him continually irritated if not raging. He has some slight release in his frequent murderous daydreams, where in Walter Mitty - like fantasies he visualizes himself dropping down on one knee to fire his bazooka into the White House or imagines himself driving a hot harpoon into McGinley's neck or "driving in slowly behind Stanley Krannick, husband to Luella, bad father to the late Junie, nudging him behind the knees so that he'll fall forward and be gently ground to death beneath Brown's Goodrich tires" (p. 243).[5]

It is not all fantasy. He acts as well. A "spirit of daily service" had remained with him from his seminary training, and "he performed every day an anonymous deed for justice" (p. 4).[6] These take mainly the form of anonymous letters or anonymous phone calls, in which he sometimes merely gives malefactors his judgment of them, addressing, for example, letters to former President Johnson as "Greatest Mass Murderer of Recent Time" (pp. 18 - 19), but in which he sometimes takes more direct action, as in the letter to Stanley Krannick where he pretends to be with the child welfare agency and sends Krannick off in terror.

"He wished above all to be productive, to improve the world. Had he done so? Had he made the world in any way better? He had saved some souls, especially children's, by writing threatening or abusive anonymous letters here and there" (p. 4); but essentially the world seemed to him to go on as rottenly as before, Junie dead, and Johnson and atom-bomb murderer Truman alive and famous, McGinley about to become congressman.

It would be too much to bear if it were not for his prim and modest "wife," Luella. With her "magic hands" she massages the rage out of his system, "drawing his rage from him into her own hands, making his rage her own" (p. 29), "lightening his heart of the burden of Junie's death, relieving Brown of the burden of revenge" (p. 60).

For if he legislated the law, she saw to it that it was executed. "Luella appeared to Brown to be without fantasies, without nonsense . . . she was all business, no pipedreams, no daydreams, no castles in the air, no murder a day to keep her doctor away, no morning anger. You couldn't have two dreamers in one house; you needed one hard head at least, and that was Luella" (pp. 61 - 62). Brown does not realize how accurate he is, for of course she keeps everything from him, and he thinks of her only as a lovely, but sometimes foolish, woman, wearing her McGinley button, for instance, only because McGinley had flattered her. "He was big on words," Luella thinks of Brown, "but that was just his trouble, too big on words and small on deeds, whereas, as far as *she* was concerned, she didn't much care what she said so long as she did what she did" (p. 55).[7]

While Brown is judging men corrupt, she is taking direct steps, massaging the rage out of his hands, massaging it back into Berberick, who is shortly to murder McGinley in just the manner Brown had always fantasized murdering Krannick, "nudging him behind the knees" with the car. And this scarcely achieved, she has begun working on Officer Phelps, convincing him that Stanley Krannick has no right to live.

V   *Brown as Writer*

As we have seen repeatedly, the protagonists of Harris's novels tend to be writers: Willie Jim, the black novelist of *Trumpet to the World;* Vachel Lindsay, an actual writer in the novelized biography *City of Discontent;* "Author" Wiggen of the three baseball novels; Lee Youngdahl of *Wake Up, Stupid;* Westrum of *The Goy* (also Harris himself in the autobiographical works *Mark the Glove Boy* and *Twentyone Twice*). *Killing Everybody*, at first sight so different from Harris's other works, once more has a writer protagonist, and again, one who in some ways represents Harris himself. But the "disguise" in this case is thoroughgoing, the connection remote; and further, the "protagonist" is displaced from the center of the novel, having a role no greater than many other characters. Nonetheless, in the character of Brown, Harris makes his most searching analysis yet of the role of the writer.

Brown, like Harris himself, and many other writers, must do something else to make a living. Brown writes headlines for the *Chronicle*. He takes a certain pride of craftsmanship in his work ("I've written some nice heads in my time"—[p. 14]), and his profession has its influences on the shape of his mind, for he often thinks of events in terms of the headlines he would write for them. But it is not where his heart is. "Brown had once intended to become a writer and save the world, but events hadn't worked that way." He must learn, as Harris and Lee Youngdahl learned before him, that if he wants to earn his bread by writing, he can only do it by writing to some mythical lowest common denominator. He "had been a most excellent writer at Faith Calvary Central, and in the end been rebuked for his skill, for Dr. Blikey told him that his essays were 'too literary . . . too profound,' that the qualities truly valued in 'this modern world of ours,' as Dr. Blikey phrased it, were 'straight talk, easy sentences, direct thought, and only one thought to one sentence' " (pp. 13 - 14). So in the end he had had to appear before the world as headline-writer, as another might appear as teacher, and on his own time devote himself to his real calling.

As anonymous letter-writer, he from his very first attempt finds himself involved in the complexities and delights of fiction writing. He had gone to the child welfare agency to complain about the treatment little Junie was receiving from his father, but there a black man wearing cracked spectacles had told him they were so overworked and understaffed (the office staff, as he said this, was lounging around drinking coffee) that he doubted they could get to it for several weeks. He decides to take the law into his own hands, and stealing a sheaf of letterhead stationery from the office, he writes a threatening letter to Stanley Krannick. He no sooner writes the letter than he realizes he must sign it. But what signature shall he put?

Why not initials? Even initials would suffice. Yet even initials required arrangement, and arrangement required invention, and that was it: inventing. He had never learned to invent because he had never been permitted to invent. He was of an austere parentage bent upon truth and facts, and he was only beginning to learn here, now, at this age, perhaps from Luella, for example, and certainly from students, artists, and rakes he met during the

course of his journalist's day, how to change or transpose reality toward the
end of improving life, how to *imagine*.

Then he saw before him the black man with the cracked spectacles.
McCracken Black. There was a name! . . . He signed the mailing copy of
his letter, and he addressed the envelope.

To have invented a name! True, he had only gone from Brown to Black,
and yet, for Brown, this was a tremendous breakthrough, a most satisfying
departure from his past—to have been able to introduce the existence of a
non-existent creature, to have manufactured a man out of his own mind;
this was godlike and uplifting; and now, to alter events, too, that would also
be satisfying, uplifting, and most godlike of all, for Brown would force
Stanley to cease his cruelty to Junie, and thus rescue a child (pp. 49 - 50).

What is interesting is that in this latest and most mature statement by Harris of his art, there is a suspicious element of impurity,
of art as kinetic, of art which has its justification in its eventuating
in action. Is this a falling away from the stern aesthetic of "what
matters is how well you write, how truly, not what you write
about"? It seems to me Harris deals very subtly and perhaps
profoundly with the issue, and that rather than going back to his
first youthful position, to Vachel Lindsay's "the sermon and the
proclamation are the important thing"—he has rather gone forward
to a new position, which insists that *yes*, the art is the important
thing, the end—but nonetheless, if the art is right, then something
else happens, something beyond. If no major change is brought
about, in small ways the world is improved. In a book written a few
years before *Killing Everybody*, Harris was discussing the just-dead
T. S. Eliot. Starting with the idea that "Shelley once called poets
the unacknowledged legislators of the world," he went on to say,
"In pushing forward in literature, T. S. Eliot . . . dragged the
United States forward politically. He accomplished this by in-
creasing our powers of perception, teaching us to see better, showing us a wasteland where we hadn't known one existed. Finally
these perceptions of the unacknowledged legislators drift down to
the acknowledged legislators."[8]

McGinley, only a few minutes before he will be murdered,
notices Brown hanging around his headquarters, and looks at him
suspiciously. " 'He's harmless,' said Officer Phelps in a professional
tone, but he instantly regretted his callousness; how little to say of a
man with "a sophisticated moral code' " (p. 250). Brown has no
such sense of harmlessness himself, feeling "if he weren't careful
things would erupt, for by the commission of acts however

harmless, or even by the private invisible commission of thoughts themselves, vibrations emanate and become suggestions. Someone should lock him up" (p. 112). Indeed, we find later that Brown has "put a good idea" in Lala's head, and she begins to contemplate a career of writing anonymous letters, first of all one to Christopher's parents. And later still, we find Berberick murdering McGinley in just the manner of one of Brown's fantasies. But by this time, Brown has stopped worrying about moral responsibility in his writing: "*A true artist*" he writes, "*bears no responsibility for the actions he inspires. Your obligation is only to tell the truth of your feelings*" (p. 247).

VI *The Reversal of Morality*

Though pacifism is often a theme in Harris's novels, only in *Something About a Soldier* (1957) and *Killing Everybody* (1973) is it central. It is interesting to compare the means of embodying this theme in the two novels.

In *Something About a Soldier* there are the good characters, Jacob, Dodd, and Joleen, who essentially are passive victims of the cold, impersonal system which is training young boys to kill, then sending them off to their deaths in the name of some abstraction like The World. Their only means of fighting this impersonal force is through love, not of The World, but of each other. Dodd, Christlike, sacrifices his own life to save Jacob for Joleen, whom he calls "Love," putting himself as lamb in the way of the knife meant for Jacob. Jacob can resist only by refusing to fight, by laying down his arms and walking away. Joleen, not as an abstract but as a personal, physical love, gives Jacob the motivation to refuse killing and death in order to survive for her. Nathan the Communist, filled with bitterness and hate because of his suffering under the system, believes in war as an answer to injustice, believes Hitler as murderer of Jews and socialists must be destroyed. In the novel it is made clear he is a good person who has been misguided, and it is a vital step in Jacob's development when he breaks free of Nathan's martial influence and listens to his heart instead of his mind.

In short, almost everyone in the novel is a victim. The system itself is only seen indirectly, in the advertisements in *Life*, which over and over again suggest that war is good for business.

As we have seen, far from mellowing, Harris has moved toward stronger and stronger statement. In *Killing Everybody*, the system has been personified in certain evil men, evil because money and possessions are of more value to them than human life, even the lives of those closest to them, their own wives and children. And, with an objective evil facing them, the victims have become less passive. Even Jacob, in *Something About a Soldier*, had been passive only to a degree. "While it might, he felt, be agreeable or desirable to kill a German who had earlier killed Jews, it was somewhat excessive to kill the first German he met without inquiring into that *particular* German's views" (p. 115). It is the impersonality, the inaccuracy, of abstract system versus abstract system which is the evil of war. Personal vengeance is another thing. There are actual evil persons in the world who should not live, and the "good" characters in *Killing Everybody* work with pinpoint accuracy to destroy them.

What is striking about the novel is Harris's designation of who are the good characters, and who the bad. War for profit, the killing of young men in order to enrich or entertain old men, is made so great an evil in the novel, that every conventional form of sinfulness becomes positive good in comparison. This is the novel's boldest stroke.

There are the obvious evil people in the novel: on the immediate personal level Stanley Krannick, who tortured his infant son for amusement, and McGinley, who as head of the draft board played with young men's lives for profit; and on a more remote level, former Presidents Johnson and Truman, both responsible for thousands of deaths in Asia. More surprising, perhaps, as bad guys, are those denominated here, as in *The Goy*, "moral neutrals," those with the power to act, and yet who do not. Among these are the astronauts, diverting attention from earth to space (p. 244), and in particular, Walter Cronkite, whose handling of the news is severely criticized: "Junie died because nobody worried enough. Cronkite the messenger called warriors 'advisors' long after they had ceased to be advisors and had certainly become warriors, though he must have known better, but cared too little for precision or religion or devotion, or couldn't afford it, and anyhow the point was to hold your audience, make a show, amuse the commuter, entertain the family digesting, don't bother their heads, keep it moving, make it fast, make it lively, faster, faster, compete, speed it up, whereas precision slowed you down, worrying slowed you down" (p. 243). Cronkite's fault, interestingly, is that he is a hack, that he cares too little for craftsmanship, and in the end this has made him an "accomplice" (p. 18). For if, as we have seen, the poets are legislators, the hacks are—to keep the parallel straight—demagogues. (Although an ex-journalist himself, Harris has never had anything good to say about journalism.[9])

For good people, we have Brown, who is one of those who makes anonymous threats by phone or letter; lustful mass-murderer Berberick; adulteress and child-molester Lala; and Luella, with her illegal massage parlor where she performs obscene acts in return for murders. Every sexual relationship is illicit in one way or another: Brown's with Luella, Lala's with Berberick and Christopher, are adulterous; Luella forms obvious mother-son relationships with Berberick and Phelps, customers at her massage parlor; Lala takes thirteen-year-old Christopher maternally and sexually to her breast. And if this is not enough, most of the sexual acts themselves are other than straight intercourse.

Thus the novel's strongest statement, and inescapably its biggest, if perhaps most savage, joke, is that every kind of conventional immorality in comparison to the institutionally sanctioned mass murder of war becomes positive moral excellence, life-force against life-denial.

VII   *The New Synthesis*

Inspection shows us that this novel, in many ways unlike all Harris's previous novels, is in fact a new synthesis of elements from his past work. His signature is everywhere. The protagonist as writer is seen, mutedly, in Brown the anonymous letter-writer, who like Lee and Harris before him must learn the disadvantages of craft, that only the sloppy hack can achieve commercial success. There is the almost obligatory reading of an actual *Life* magazine, not only as it reflects most directly all that is shallow and despicable in our culture, but also as a sort of culminatory pun on Harris's constant attempt to interfuse fiction with "life." There is the old theme of woman, standing in the background, but always acting powerfully on the men, either as stabilizing influence—Holly or Beth or Beatrice (in *The Goy*), or as glamorous sexual temptress—Patricia Moors or Katie, the whore in *Bang the Drum Slowly*, or Gabriella Bodeen or "Madame" in *The Goy*. It is interesting that as the stabilizer and the temptress progress through the novels, they more and more grow to be the same person, so that finally, in *Killing Everybody*, Luella becomes both, domestic refuge for Brown,

femme fatale to Berberick and Phelps. She even tempts them in the
same manner that Katie the whore had tempted Henry
Wiggen—with a lifetime pass to her establishment. Again we see
the motif of man under stress, lashing out misguidedly at his friends
rather than his enemies. This motif began as a slight statement with
the young man who is not making the team at spring tryouts
suddenly attacking Henry in *The Southpaw*, the players themselves
turning on one another when the going gets tough, even Henry, under stress, throwing a dangerous—possibly murderous—"spitter" at
a perfectly likable person on the other team. It becomes more
prominent in *Wake Up, Stupid* as Lee, suffering from nerves, takes
his play manuscript away from Paul Purdy, or plays thoughtless
pranks on Outerbridge, or threatens to step out on his wife; and
more central still in *The Goy*, where Westrum, under stress, actually
cripples his son for life. But the development culminates, perhaps,
with Berberick murdering "left and right" in the stress of combat.

Also, once again in this novel we see the anarchic gesture—so
closely related to the lashing-out-at-friends as to be almost inex-
tricable from it, and yet often coming as a prelude to revelation.
Here, certainly, it has become positive, a channelling of destructive
forces into constructive action: "Take the law into his own hands?
Certainly Brown would not have done so had the law appeared to
function. He began to feel that he had not only a right but a *duty* to
take the law into his own hands" (p. 43). So also with Luella and
finally with Berberick, whose aimless slaughter under stress is converted into accurate murder aimed against his actual oppressor.

We have already discussed—or touched upon—standard Harris
themes in this novel, but I wish to stress the difference, the new
orientation, the new synthesis. In the 1965 interview with John
Enck, Harris had tentatively predicted that he might "finally be
through with myself as the disguised person in my books and then
move into a pure form of either fiction or non-fiction." This appears
to be what he has done in *Killing Everybody*. By removing himself
to the vantage of an omniscient author and eliminating a central
character with whom he is obviously to be identified, he has deper-
sonalized himself into the form and structure of the novel; his standard characters are reshuffled, redistributed, so that if something of
himself as writer remains in Brown, other characters too share these
qualities—Lala, who conceives herself to be a poet and plans to em-
bark on her own anonymous letter-writing campaign, as well as

Berberick, who has already written a few letters. The lashing out against friends shifts away from Brown to Berberick; the anarchic gesture, centralized in Luella, spreads out over all of them. And each, formerly corrupted or betrayed by what is worst in himself or his culture, in coming of age finds his true role, which is not to be a slave or a possession or a pander, but rather to join freely in love with all others who share his life-force and to unite in the destruction of the life-deniers.

CHAPTER 7

The Autobiographical Interlude: Friedman & Son, Mark the Glove Boy, *and* Twentyone Twice

I T seemed best to me to deal with all of Harris's novels one after the other. Now I would like to back up in time to the long decade (1959 - 70) between *Wake Up, Stupid* and *The Goy* when Harris was writing no novels.

His major book-length publications of this period were: *Friedman & Son* (1963), a play which might be described as an autobiographical fantasy and which was printed with an autobiographical introduction nearly as long as the play; and *Mark the Glove Boy* (1964) and *Twentyone Twice* (1966), two autobiographical works "carved" out of Harris's journal. The play, of course, is a created fictional work and will be discussed as such; but the two autobiographical volumes as well can be discussed almost as novels. As might be expected from an author who shaded his novels into biography, his autobiographies shade into his novels. They are slighter productions, perhaps, but they contain many of the same elements and motifs, and almost inevitably selection has given them a novelistic shape and unity.

The three works, in addition to dealing with Harris's personal experience more directly than any of his other printed volumes, bear another curious similarity. Each is divided into two parts, the second a commissioned or public part, the first an explanation, a justification for, the writing of the second. The curious thing is that the justification is as long and full (in one case infinitely longer and fuller) than the thing it is justifying. If we take this as a hint that Harris perhaps protests too much, it begins to be possible to see a connection between these works and the long hiatus in his novel-writing.

I   *The Price of Consent*

At any rate, when a writer writes seven novels during one decade, and none at all the following decade, turning instead into close autobiographical probing of motives, we would suspect some sort of creative or personal crisis even had Harris not spoken quite candidly about one in the introduction to *Friedman & Son.*

His problem—he suggests there—is double, a double burden of guilt gradually becoming one in his mind. First, he had been estranged from his father, and his father died suddenly before they could make it up. Second, after a lifetime of attacking society in his writing, he sees that society turn around and reward him with money and honors and he feels himself being seduced and corrupted, fears he is joining the conspiracy he had sought to destroy. "That summer—1959, my father's last summer, when we broke off—my emptiness had begun to worry me. I was composed and mellow, and the living was easy. All that had been on my mind I had discharged in a novel, *Wake Up, Stupid*, published in July, and so successful in its way that it was soon to carry me beyond accustomed comforts" (p. 13).[1]

He had watched his novel go through several printings, and then "Playhouse 90" sent him $7,500 just for considering doing an adaptation of the novel for television. He also had $5,000 to do a script of *Bang the Drum Slowly* for Broadway. The Ford Foundation gave him an additional $7,500 to free him to work on his plays. "I could now count," he observes, "$20,000 for plays for which no actor had ever been cast: the wry observation that in America some writers live well enough on grants and options began to assume for me a certain reality" (p. 38). *Esquire* called him up and asked him to take part in a symposium at Iowa with Norman Mailer and others ($500), and another symposium in San Francisco. The National Institute of Arts sent him $2,000 for "ongoing literary creation" (p. 58), and he was appointed to be on the San Francisco Arts Commission by a mayor who "had never read my work but certainly intended to" (p. 53). He was even, on the strength of his novel, invited to be on Groucho Marx's "You bet Your Life," where he won an additional $1,050.

"I consented to this, as I was cheerfully consenting to almost everything those days. It is a dangerous game" (p. 20). The "Playhouse 90" people had warned him that he was not to make Irwin, the boxer in *Wake Up, Stupid*, a "dumb Negro" lest they get

the NAACP on their backs. "The public image of the Negroes was
now in my custody. What an opportunity, eh? I could make a
Renaissance man out of a Negro boxer if I care to, and beam it out
for ninety minutes to helpless millions. . . . But was it truthful?
Was there any really good reason why a Negro boxer couldn't be
well educated, soft-spoken, decent, upstanding, and a killer too? All
I needed to do was consent" (pp. 16 - 17). And he found himself
striving, in his script of *Bang the Drum Slowly*, for a "theatrical
reality" which would work on Broadway, just as for the television
script he was "straining for a clarity unnatural to life as I knew it,
however natural it may appear to the proprietors of television, or to
the audience" (p. 19).

Along with all his monetary successes there is a steady under-
current. "I am beginning to wonder about myself [as a writer]: it is
two full years since my last hard labor" (p. 41). "I was now two and
a half years since I had written anything large" (p. 68). What was
blocking him?

He received his first clue at the Iowa symposium, from Norman
Mailer.

Just before lunch Mailer had arrived, baggy and shaggy, up all night in
Chicago, needing a shave, and smelling bad. Luncheon was lavish on white
cloth, and the service was impeccable, not a crime in itself but tending to
introduce a note of propriety and formality—the suffocating tone of a
gentlemen's club of exactly the sort whose rules excluded Jews, unless, of
course, they were good Jews, white Jews, anti-Semitic Jews, knew the rules
and kept them, and at last bred Jewishness out of themselves and out of
their line. Of course it wasn't the case, only my reflex. . . . Mailer . . .
looked *at* me, and I felt overdressed and overshorn and overbathed,
costumed for the masquerade, hidden, hiding, something in me going the
wrong way as it had been for some months, a little genteel now, my accent
not quite my own—" (pp. 25 - 26).

When they discuss later the talks they gave at the symposium,
Harris accuses Mailer of having been incoherent; Mailer accuses
Harris of having been dull and safe. "He had caught me hiding,
safely reading, not giving, purified of risk, canned, faking a high IQ
when I was not intellect but religion, feigning coherence, dressed as
a professor at the respectable masquerade. *Something I was
withholding.* He didn't say what" (p. 27).

Whether actually divining something in Mailer's attitude, or
simply projecting into Mailer's incoherence his own self-doubts, he

seemed to receive a message. "Something must be made of it, but I don't know what—he wanted to establish, I suppose, that there was something he knew that I didn't . . . wanted to tell me he'd been somewhere I hadn't, crashed upon the rocks in the place he'd been, undone, unstrung, wrecked, battered, lost himself, hidden himself from himself, because that's what they take from you in return for your consent, promising you everything you thought you wanted. They had buried him beneath rewards, he'd been a decade trying to dig his way out, it might be another before he was up and free, and meanwhile he was appalled at my ridiculous eagerness to tumble into the trap" (p. 28).

II *"Something I Was Withholding"*

Harris was still puzzling over what it was Màiler thought he might be hiding, when a woman friend commented to him (looking at a series of photographs recently taken at a faculty gathering) that in all but one "my face was as she seemed to see it day by day, but in the single . . . exception, she said, it 'looks Jewish.' Seen in a certain light at a certain angle it produced an image hitherto hidden. *Of course I am* (says Ferguson, son of Friedman), *it's stamped on everything I've ever written*. But was it? Or was there always sufficient ambiguity, a camouflage of name and face by which I hoped to have and have not, be and not be, a method of entering the gentlemen's club I claimed I despised? The loss of Jewish identity had been the theme of the single book of mine which had interested Mailer. Perhaps he thought it the best clue to my going on" (pp. 29 - 30).

At this moment, when he feels he has bought his success at the cost of denying his heritage (most obviously symbolized by his having dropped his father's Finkelstein from his name, just as his character Ferguson changes his name from his father's Friedman), news comes of his father's death.

And soon Harris has a new betrayal to worry about. He had been asked to do an essay on young writers for the *New York Times Book Review*. News had just come that Norman Mailer had stabbed his wife, and Harris was annoyed "by the smug reactions to Mailer's calamity. Some writers whose vulnerabilities he had exposed behaved as if his scandal necessarily exonerated them of theirs" (p. 50). So Harris began his essay with a long quotation by Mailer in which Mailer asserted the writer should be a bold revolutionary.

Harris, taking his tone from Mailer, in his essay accused the new younger writers of being cowardly and safe.

The *Times Book Review* editor wrote back that he must delete his first paragraphs. Among other things, it "is a mistake to start any literary paper at the moment with a quote from poor Norman Mailer." " 'If you want simply an orthodox little essay,' I wrote, 'I wonder why you ask me.' Nevertheless, I consented. Brave noises, followed by consent, that's me" (p. 52).

Is it all of a piece, the attempts to write for popular mass culture, with all the seductions this offers, the consent it entails—and the rejection of the inconvenient Jewish name, in order to enter the great white Protestant gentlemen's club of America? Robert Frost's lines (from "The Gift Outright") come to him: "Something we were withholding made us weak / Until we found out that it was ourselves" (p. 57).

III   *The Undesirability of Assimilation*

"Society, that enemy always goading me to labor, now threatened, by taking me in, to deprive me of my inspiration" (p. 14).

The insight comes that his weakness, his minority status, is his strength, forcing him into an antagonistic position, disciplining and refining his sense of moral outrage, stiffening and giving shape to his creative resolve. He remembers when he was a child his close friendship with an Irish Catholic boy, two minorities in a WASP world who shared another disability as well:

Our small stature was our first identity, for he or I was always least, and therefore last in line, and the other second. We bore our humiliation, vowing not revenge but justice. If Society thought us small, and assigned us the lowest place, we knew what Society was: it was blind and stupid. This much we told ourselves, and spun out of our first disadvantage a theory of the world whose basis was outrage and whose goal was remedy. What a great profit is loss! What a great fortune is misfortune! Our sense of justice was early born (p. 18).

Harris was reaching now the age where as he walked up to a building, the distorting reflection of windows mirrored back to him his father's shape and walk and gesture. Looking through his dead father's papers, he is "shattered" at the variety, the energy, the art. The rhythms of the prose, the very pointing of the sentences, are his today. Amidst the cartons of papers he inherits he finds the documents of vast and endless years-long litigation between his lawyer father and the state, "that single case at law, that magnum opus of my father, that Great American Novel, that Epic Poem, his burden, his hope, his curse, that last stand which tried his moral intelligence, produced his ultimate joy and his ultimate exasperation, and which defined his ceaseless conflict with Society" (p. 48).

His immigrant grandfather had had no English, and so English, the language itself, the words, so hard bought, became very special to his father, and to Harris, too. A character in *Friedman & Son* very suggestively says: "Consider the Department of English of our famous University, where Jewish boys whose fathers could barely speak the language teach the sons and the daughters of the first families of the *Mayflower* how to make a little bit of sense in English" (p. 86). A sort of final revelation comes to Harris when he is watching the Rome Olympics on television: "Most of what the U.S. took our Negroes took for us. Here were passion and desire in bursting lungs. Break the tape and you win more than a medal: you win new neighborhoods. But what would happen when all was integrated? Where would the next fresh wave of American energy come from once all the strains were assimilated, all the desire or all the immigrant memory erased? The thought moved me. Assimilation was not impossible but undesirable" (p. 47).

From this revelation the concentric circles continue to develop and widen. For he is a minority not only in size, in Jewishness, but in his very craft as artist, his concern for words in a culture careless of words or meanings, his integrity and intellect in a world embarrassed by both. He gives up Broadway, television scripts, and writes his own play, with its concern for language, precision, compression, which deals as truly as he can with his Jewishness, and at the same time presents Jews warm and human, and Jews as swindling, calculating, and money-grubbing. For just as all Negroes aren't intellectual, Ferguson in the play reminds us, "All Jews aren't honest. We range the human scale. If you say we're all honest you deprive us of our humanity" (p. 136):

The translation of my memory into meaning, and the unification of so large an action within such small time, require a compression likely to challenge many persons beyond their training or their patience. For a writer who, like *this* one, yearns to address all Americans and all the world with a single emancipating breath, the fact of the essential privacy of meticulous literature is a disappointing reality. But neither the one straight line of television nor the theatrical reality demanded by Broadway can serve. We know too much (p. 60).

IV   Friedman & Son

The play begins in the studio of Ferguson (born Friedman), a well-known writer. Ferguson and his father have not spoken for four and one-half years. An unabridged dictionary, a present from his father, lies tattered on the floor, stepped on, kicked, played with by the children, a stand to put the dog's bowl on. Daily envelopes sent by the father containing clippings cut out of various newspapers and having to do (we find out later) with changes in word usage are thrown unopened into the wastebasket.

Despite desecrating the dictionary and the etymological messages of his father, Ferguson as a writer is very much a man of words and very particular about how they are used. His wife, getting ready to go out, says, "Button me up, please. FERGUSON: I'll *zip* you up. KATHLEEN: Well, whatever's there, do it, dear? FERGUSON: A zipper is not a button, a button is not a zipper" (pp. 70 - 71).

To his annoyance, just when his writing is going well, Schimmel enters. Schimmel, as his character develops in the play, is a virtual stage kike, speaking in *oy vey* dialect, measuring everything in terms of how much money it can be converted into. He quickly runs afoul of Ferguson in his use of language. Asked what his business is, he says, "I am not on business. I am simply an ambassador from your father" (p. 73). But when a few moments later he says, "Frankly speaking, if I had a chair I could transact my business better. FERGUSON: I thought you weren't on business. SCHIMMEL: Your ear catches every little word. FERGUSON: That's my business. What's your business?" (p. 75).

Schimmel makes his living staging (at considerable expense to his customer) gaudy testimonial dinners. "Last night I arranged a testimonial dinner for a man with all the personal integrity of a—tiger. This morning he is looked upon as the son of Florence Nightingale by Albert Schweitzer" (p. 79).

He has come to the studio to suggest that for one thousand dollars he will set up a testimonial dinner for Ferguson's father. Ferguson tells him it is ridiculous: "The whole concept of my father embarrasses me. SCHIMMEL: A father is not a concept. A father is a man of blood and bones. You also are a father. Your father is a highly respected man throughout the city. He has a character. FERGUSON: Yes, but it's a defective character" (p. 81).

But Schimmel, for all that he is gross and mercenary, is by no means stupid. He has easily worked out that Ferguson wants to be reunited with his father. When Ferguson claims his father has stopped talking to him, Schimmel shrewdly asserts that it is Ferguson who has stopped talking to his father. When he scolds Ferguson for mistreating the dictionary which has been his father's gift of words to him, Ferguson says he has no need for it, he makes up his own words.

"SCHIMMEL: You don't use a dictionary, you make up all your own words, all very clever, be as clever as you please, tell yourself you made your success all by yourself, nobody helped you; but tell yourself that, and you lie. Excellent, you may lie to yourself, but don't lie to me, I'm too smart. Give a little credit to your father's pride and stubbornness, they helped you" (p. 96). And then in the play's longest speech he reminds Ferguson in no uncertain terms of the Jewish heritage he had been seeking to deny:

Words are hard come by. In the house of the son of an immigrant the dictionary is the whole connection to life. No such trial and tribulation was ever known to mankind so great as the question of words in the house of the son of an immigrant. You wake up in the morning in Russian, how are you feeling in Yiddish, it's time to go to work in English. *You* may go about shortening your name from Friedman to Ferguson, but still in your every bone you are a Jew the son of a Jew in turn the son of a Jew back to Moses. . . . Don't be so smug, my dear young Ferguson, not simply to pester you with mental exercises does your father bring to your kind attention the latest meaning of words. The father of your father knew no English. Perhaps your father has no such defective character as you may think (p. 97).

The completely crushed Ferguson can only say, "He'll never come." "I'll go to see him now," Schimmel replies.

In Act Two, Schimmel arrives at old Friedman's apartment. It is, in the objects it contains, noticeably similar to Ferguson's studio. And Friedman, just as his son, is critically conscious of the meaning of words. The scene, in fact, closely parallels Act One. The first thing Friedman does is attack Schimmel's word usage.

Schimmel tells him that his son summoned him to his house to ask him to arrange a testimonial dinner for his father. Friedman is obviously delighted to hear this, but he wants to know if Schimmel was summoned to his son's house, or merely went.

"*Summoned*, or *went*, a needless quibble is a waste of effort," Schimmel says (p. 106).

However, after a long discussion, Friedman finally catches

Schimmel lying red-handed and calls him a liar. But just as in the first act, Schimmel wheels adroitly and catches Friedman in his own lie. Just as he had caught Ferguson trying to deny his Jewish past, he now catches Friedman for pretending that there has been no rupture between him and his dutiful son: "Careful, Friedman, who you are so quick to call a liar. You have not spoken to your son in four and a half years" (p. 113). Friedman is stricken. Schimmel easily convinces the broken, hesitant old man to come with him to his son's studio.

Act Three opens with Schimmel and Friedman knocking at Ferguson's door. Ferguson frantically hides the abused dictionary, the unopened letters. Schimmel comes in, brings them together. "SCHIMMEL: Victory. My mission is accomplished, a small, simplified contract is by no means amiss [he is still pushing for the testimonial dinner]" (p. 113). It does not go quite that smoothly. They are stiff with each other at first, though reconciliation obviously is well on the way, when once more the difference of words comes up. When Schimmel brings up "the proposition you summoned me to discuss":

FERGUSON *(To Friedman):* I never summoned him.
FRIEDMAN: He said you summoned him. . . .
FERGUSON: It is always crucial to tell the truth.
SCHIMMEL: Don't mix in any little white lies, just because a father's heart is at stake (p. 126).

But he will not, and father and son, in their pride of being champions of exact truth, are on the point of separating again. Schimmel, with diabolical cleverness, is still in control. He says, no wonder your son won't give you a dinner, he hates you. "He finds your character defective. So he said. FRIEDMAN *(To Ferguson):* You said such a thing?" (p. 130). We heard him say it and know he did not mean it, but his motives for having said it, compounded out of pride, guilt, and an effort at self-deception, are too complicated ever to be explained to his father. "Certainly not," he lies, and Schimmel has him. He is forced to say that he uses the dictionary ("It was my father's gift to me. FRIEDMAN: Hundreds of thousands of words. Any word he might need, there it was in my gift to him"—[p. 129]) and that he opens all the envelopes and reads them every day ("FRIEDMAN: Until I have prepared an envelope for you I do not feel that my day has begun"—[p. 131]).

Now Schimmel has him indeed, suddenly discovering and producing the tattered dictionary and the unopened envelopes. "Tell me who is a liar. How do you possibly open every envelope, my dear young man, when all are sealed? Sealed is sealed, sealed is not opened, ha, ha, ha, every envelope a bullet in your father's heart. Die, Friedman, die" (p. 131). He leaves, scowling with contempt, but returns in an instant, smiling, when Ferguson shouts that now he is ready to sign a contract.

V "It Would Have Freed You Financially"

These dramatic confrontations and reversals, intricately patterned and cleverly timed, are only the first level of the play's treatment of the different kinds of truth-telling and lies. Schimmel (whose name in German—the basis of Yiddish—means "mildew" or "mouldy") comes to stand for that mass culture which thrives on spectacle, however vulgar, asking only that it be simple, not confusing to the least intellect, holding to the safest clichés, avoiding the appropriate taboos, and above all not pausing over words or worrying overmuch about their meanings. As businessman, he stands as spokesman for those other representatives of society he can conjure up at will and bring upon the stage, who for a price will make standard speeches of praise at his testimonial dinners: the Mayor, the Judge, the General, the Assistant Superintendent of Schools, the New York Book Publisher.

All these but the last, it turns out, have been engaged in a long conspiracy against Friedman. Masking themselves under the corporate name of the "Federated—Something—Synagogues" they are trying to buy a choice piece of land he owns in the center of the city, on which, rather than building a synagogue, they mean actually "to build a beautiful parking lot, a decoration to the city, an immense circular garage" (p. 74). They have offered him twice the price he wanted, but he will not sell. "It wasn't that I didn't want the money. Look, I'm no complainer, I'm no statute of moral cleanliness carved in Ivory Soap, but don't think I'm so dumb I don't know the meaning of a simple word. I have my pride. A parking lot is not a synagogue, a synagogue is not a parking lot, in one you pray, in the other you park. . . . schimmel: It would have freed you financially" (pp. 139 - 40)—but at the cost of selling out his principles, his allegiance to the word. In the end they take him to court (the judge—one of the co-conspirators—hearing the case),

and since they have nothing to get him on, they finally put him in
jail for contempt, which he does indeed have for them, calling them
all stinkers.

When Schimmel suggests these very men as speakers at the
testimonial dinner, Friedman refuses absolutely to have them.
Instead, he asks to have his son's publisher, believing that here was
one part of Society still uncorrupt. But we quickly find that the
publisher is as much a part of the conspiracy as the others. For he
tells us that one day he had outlined a book for Ferguson to write
"which I then believed, and still believe, would capture the
American fancy as nothing had done since Abie's Irish
Rose. . . . It would have freed him financially. FERGUSON: But im-
prisoned me in other ways" (pp. 137 - 38). Since Ferguson, though
a Jew, had married an Irish girl, the publisher suggested that as the
starting point for the novel: "Take the Jewish boy and the Irish girl
and mix them well with the topical interest in Israel and in Ireland.
[The play was written before the present topical interest in these
countries.] I sent him to Israel, and to Ireland. Soak up the at-
mosphere, I said. Then come home and give us the season's biggest
book. He raised questions, and I answered them. How should he
treat the Jews? Favorably. How should he treat the Irish?
Favorably. How should he treat the Arabs? Unfavorably. Give us, I
said, a book as heartwarming as Jewish family life, as lively as an
Irish jig, as red and as white and as blue as a *(groping for the image)*
Presidential Inauguration. In tone be topical, be direct, be simple,
don't confuse your reader, don't linger over words, words don't
matter. . ." (p. 138).

Like father, like son, they find now they have both resisted the
temptation of financial freedom in order to preserve the sanctity of
the word, and with it their own integrity.

VI   *"Crucial to Tell the Truth"*

But Ferguson and Friedman have also had to learn that the
relationship between truth and the word is not simple. Schimmel,
we have seen, tells either truth or lies, whichever at the moment
best serves his mercenary end. For instance, when he produces the
sealed envelopes, it is "truth," but used only as a means to extort a
contract for a dinner out of Ferguson. And so mere truth is not
always sufficient. As Schimmel himself is fond of saying, "Please,
pay no attention to the words, grasp the spirit of the occasion" (p.

85). We see many places in the play where, in fact, a lie is the most direct way of approaching the truth. Ferguson's wife has seen this from the start, for when Ferguson accuses her of having called his father, she replies, "Didn't you want me to? You tell me so often not to I can only conclude you want me to" (p. 69).

Ferguson's pride—a pride he inherits from his father—is his strength against temptation, but perhaps it is only in this indirect way a proud man can begin seeking for a reconciliation. Similarly his father, in his pride, talks to Schimmel as though there has been no estrangement, and it is not until Schimmel cruelly breaks him down and forces him to admit it that he can allow himself to be led to his son's studio.

And there, as we have already noted, Ferguson must tell direct lies as the only way of telling the truth of the heart. The word indeed is great; father and son erred only when they forgot the spirit is greater.

But greatest of all, of course, is word and spirit combined. Though never so corrupt as those around them, who honor neither, still they are divided, son from father, present from past, melting-pot American from immigrant heritage, and each within himself divides word from spirit. Their reconciliation reconciles all, and this brings about the play's final reversal.

In a moment of exuberance at the reconciliation with his father, Ferguson has told Schimmel he wants a $20,000 testimonial dinner (significantly, the amount Harris had received "for plays for which no actor had ever been cast"). Schimmel envisaged something grandiose, thousands of guests and many distinguished speakers, held at the Jack Tar Hotel, justly famous for being the most extravagantly vulgar in San Francisco.

But first father and son decide that in the speeches Ferguson must be referred to not as the famous son of Friedman, but as the famous *Jewish* son of Friedman. Schimmel says, "It has always been our policy at gatherings of such a size to omit the word *Jewish*" (p. 135). But they insist, and Schimmel, beginning to worry about the bad press, begins suggesting a smaller party, more private, perhaps exclusively Jewish. Next, rather than having an orthodox American flag for the guests at the dinner to salute in order to show America's strength growing out of its honest immigrant past, they will all pledge allegiance to a flagpole from which is hanging a pair of pants made by Ferguson's tailor grandfather, made to fit properly and to last forever. Schimmel suggests a still smaller party.

At last Ferguson gets up, to make his own testimonial speech:

My father, knowing words, but still unconfident in language, had an artist's nose for stinkers and conspiracies. Words and nose joined in me. I am the dream-boy of every speechless father, the promise that was promised when America was promised, I am what's been melting all these years in the melting pot. . . . But I must not melt too far. I must not disappear. My duty to my father is clear: To speak with the language I now possess the ancient memory of what it was not to be free, not to know the language; to cry stinker when I am invited into a conspiracy . . . to sew together with a fine, unerring stitch the private hope with the public utterance, for a man's life must last not a season but a lifetime; whenever we give less than we own we betray our nation; whenever we tell less than we know we lie. Am I going too far, Mr. Schimmel? SCHIMMEL: Go as far as you like. The farther you go the smaller it gets (pp. 150 - 51).

In fact, Schimmel is in full flight by now, as the impresarios of mass culture, Harris suggests, will always be in the face of "meticulous" and truthful art, built to last beyond the immediate season.

VII   *The Problem with* Friedman & Son

If the long introduction was in part explanation for *Friedman & Son*, it was also in part justification. I am reminded, reading it, of parts of the essay ("Easy Does It Not") in which Harris insists that *A Ticket for a Seamstitch* was turned down by *Life* because of its high art rather than for any lack of it may have had as a story. There is a bit of the same alibiing here. *Friedman & Son* ran nine performances at the San Francisco Actor's Workshop, got poor reviews, has never been produced again. Harris writes:

I was only confirmed in the play's own truth: the greater each person's perception, the more each had of style of his own, the deeper each insight, the clearer each man's (or woman's) view of his own intentions, the fewer were the obstacles lying between him and a reasonable apprehension of the action occurring onstage (p. 60).

I am pointing here to what I think is a certain stridency in Harris's defense, not that I think the play is a minor work, as *A Ticket for a Seamstitch* is, but it strikes me as something short of major. I should not overstress this. I missed seeing the play, so that I am not quite sure how it would perform. The theater craft, if a little bit predictable, is nonetheless clear and certain, and the play strikes me as really good. I almost want to say, for some reason, "unexpectedly" or "surprisingly" good. Perhaps I am remembering Garafolo, in *Wake Up, Stupid*, picking up Youngdahl from the canvas and saying, "Lee, every man to their own trade." But this does not seem, at least in any obvious way, a "novelist's" play. It is expertly constructed, the dialogue marvelously polished—nor do I mean to imply by this the play is wooden, for it is full of life. It exploits what is a real talent of Harris's, his ability to create wacky characters and put them together in confrontation scenes which twist about with wonderful humor and ultimate meaning. But it is a talent which, while it works well embedded in the matrix of a novel, perhaps does not entirely stand by itself. I suggested in chapter five that his novel *The Goy* was missing a sufficient quantity of just this kind of action. The play provides it in plenty but perhaps misses the backup strength of the novel.

VIII   Mark the Glove Boy

Mark the Glove Boy, with its hopefully premature subtitle *The Last Days of Richard Nixon*, is the slightest of the three books we will be dealing with in this chapter. But it is, as is virtually everything Harris sets his pen to, extremely readable, and has its small importance besides. It is essentially a history of the writing of an article Harris was commissioned to do for *Life* and thus deals directly with a special theme of Harris's, the relationship between a writer and his writing. It begins with a key line: "For a writer who has advanced beyond a certain stage of his life, the work itself is experience" (p. 1).[2]

Life had called him and asked him to follow the 1962 California gubernatorial campaign between "Pat" Brown and Richard Nixon and write an article on it for their upcoming "California" issue. Now, the article already written and published,[3] "the experience remains for me to convey, as I am about to do, in the ironic form of a literary object exceeding in style the object I was commissioned to produce" (p. 1).

Harris, as usual uncomfortable with abstractions, quickly managed to personalize his task. Immediately after the call from *Life* he was out driving with his family a long way from home when his car broke down. He sat helplessly on the shoulder of the highway while cars sped indifferently past. Just as he was beginning to think bitter thoughts about the callousness of humanity a man stopped, put a chain on his car, and towed Harris's car the ten miles into town, where he could have the car repaired, rescuing "not only my family . . . and me but the human race itself, just at the moment I had begun to view it as a hostile face at a speeding window" (p. 8).

This man, with "the weathered, ruddy, inelegant redness of his face, almost its ugliness, and the smile he was obliged to carry so long as he carried such a face" comes to represent for him the California citizenry; and it is for him, in the weeks ahead, he will have the responsibility of writing the article. "I thought of myself as committed now in an unexpected personal way to return favor for favor. . . . If I had been helpless on the shoulder of the road, he was helpless to defend himself against words. I would try to clarify for him, as surely as he had towed me with his chain" (p. 8).

He thinks back to his early manhood, when he had held a job as a journalist. His editor had continually pointed out to him the biases he did not even recognize himself, but which were clearly revealed in his writing, and taught him to be responsibly objective in newswriting. Now he makes a supreme effort not to like Brown, and to like Nixon, so he can give them equal and fair treatment in the article.

This is an increasingly difficult task, as the closer he comes to Nixon, the more certain he is, not only of the candidate's limited intellect, but also of his limited goals. He appears to be running with no other objective than winning in mind. While Brown is saying "children should lead decent and interesting lives" (p. 137), Nixon is recommending the extension of capital punishment, or, in a memorable quotation on education, saying, "What are our schools for . . . if not for indoctrination against Communism?" (p. 71).

At length, with the article sent off, and after it has suffered some further dilution by *Life* editors, Harris begins to fear that, after all, he has been too fair, too impartial, that he has let down his rescuer who, innocently reading his article, might still be able to go out and vote for Nixon (the article appeared a month before the election).

But afterwards (especially after Brown had won easily, thus—everyone thought—ending Nixon's political career) Harris began to feel better about it. His own literary principle had been served: had he made it a hatchet job, it would only be because he distrusted the intelligence of his audience. By being fair, by merely presenting the two men side by side, he had won the confidence of the reader, and more, by showing rather than telling, he had, after all, effectively got across the point of which was the better man. He was left "pleased with himself, too, as if by being good he had done well, or witnessed in some way something like the triumph of virtue in a naughty world" (p. 147).

IX   Twentyone Twice

This work—which belongs in this chapter by virtue of being directly autobiographical, of containing a long first part which is in essence an explanation and justification for what is written in the second part, and by occurring during the ten-year hiatus in novel-writing—nonetheless bears many affinities with *Wake Up, Stupid* and *The Goy*, the novels which enclose the decade.

First of all, the protagonist of *Twentyone Twice*—Harris himself—though not a tall, powerful athlete, is in many respects like Youngdahl and Westrum. To begin with, he is a compulsive writer. Westrum is on the fifty-thousandth page of his life-long journal. Lee, at the beginning of *Wake Up, Stupid*, a major creative work out of the way, proposes keeping a journal and sending sections of it around to his friends. Harris, as *Twentyone Twice* opens, is on the eleven-thousandth page of his journal and is in fact sending it around, installment by installment, to several of his friends. Harris, like Youngdahl and Westrum, is a college professor who is also a well-known writer. Like them, because of his fame, he is constantly being sent, for one reason or another, to various parts of the world at other people's expense. Lee was sent to New York to confer with a play producer; Westrum was sent to Washington to serve the President; Harris, in the course of *Twentyone Twice*, is sent to Japan to take part in a conference and is called by Sargent Shriver to Washington to go on a Peace Corps assignment to Africa.

The Peace Corps assignment provides the main action of the book. Harris must first of all be cleared as a security risk by the FBI. But what is meant as a routine investigation soon reveals that Harris had not only been arrested for going AWOL from the army and then been discharged as psychoneurotic, but that he had also flirted rather openly with communism. Now he must undergo long interviews with agents and a psychiatrist to see if he is both sane and patriotic.

The investigation and other events taking place during the same period constitute the first half of the book. The second half deals with the assignment he is sent on, after his clearance finally goes through. Shriver "had read *Mark the Glove Boy* and had the definite feeling that I shared with him a sense of purpose about American life, spotting me as the kind of person who could examine the work of the Peace Corps and say useful things about it" (p. 10).[4] The idea was for Harris to tour some particular country and then write up a report for "internal" circulation on how he thought the Peace Corps was working there. "I want to know the worst before anybody else in the world knows it," Shriver said, "and I want to be able to *read* it, I don't want any of that bureaucratic nonsense" (p. 10).

Harris is sent, finally, to a small African country he calls "Kongohno," which I must confess I naïvely looked up in my most recent atlas, without finding it. Presumably Harris had his own reasons for disguising the name of the country and carefully altering any identifiable details. (Let me mention, however, that Harris has written a "limited official use government document" on the Peace Corps' teaching of English in Sierra Leone—I leave the reader to make his own connections.) His mission there is to check on certain Peace Corps "risks,"—volunteers who seem to be acting erratically or improperly.

He goes to the country, meets many volunteers, speaks informally with the "risks," and returns reporting that the volunteers are all doing splendid jobs, and the "risks" possibly rather better and more imaginative jobs than the others.

X   Twentyone Twice *as Novel*

I have said that the protagonist of *Twentyone Twice* resembles the protagonists of *Wake Up, Stupid* and *The Goy*. Curiously, *Twentyone Twice* resembles the two novels in its structure as well. In both novels, the main characters are undergoing evaluation—Youngdahl for tenure, Westrum for a seat at the Center—and this external investigation is precipitating an internal one. Precisely the same thing occurs in *Twentyone Twice*. The FBI is examining Harris to see if he is reliable enough, sane enough, loyal enough to go on a mission for the government. With slightly different emphases, these are the questions Harris—who is on page 389 of the autobiography he is writing—is asking himself. He is examining his brief, youthful army career as interestedly as the FBI to see if his behavior was rational, and he is examining his present life as well to see if now that he is forty-two he has become one of those persons over thirty who cannot be trusted, or if instead he is "twice twenty-one," two men in fact, loyal to the liberalism of his youth but with more wisdom and skill and power to make it effective. And finally, can he still be relied on to take, with automatic instinct, the right (by which he means the radical-left) side of issues, or has the caution, the greater knowledge of age, the greater ability to see all sides of an issue sicklied o'er his best actions with the pale cast of thought?

When the FBI interviews him, he is reasonably cautious with his answers, since he would like to have the job. But in many ways, he is—to them—surprisingly frank and cooperative. "My tongue was loose, I was compliant, at whatever point my life is a closed book I want to open it . . . and suffer the joys and consequences, as I've been doing in all my books, getting closer and closer to myself, tracing my childhood emotions which led to my young politics and finally shaped my manhood, being as much as possible my own psychoanalyst [cp. *The Goy*] and my own confessor" (p. 30).

Whatever the FBI is finding out, his own observation is revealing things about himself which give him pause. First of all, he has been very flattered to be invited to go over to Japan for a couple of days to take part in a cultural exchange. But when he gets there, he discovers he had been selected in place of James Baldwin, for fear Baldwin would be too outspoken. He finds it very disturbing that he is considered safe, not outspoken. The whole idea, in fact, that if he takes the Peace Corps assignment, he will be on the side of authority, checking up on the "risks," is disturbing.

Just this moment the Free Speech movement begins in Berkeley, across the San Francisco Bay from where Harris teaches. He is one of several liberal thinkers and writers in the area asked to sign a statement of support for the students, which will be printed in the *San Francisco Chronicle*, and he finds himself hanging fire. If his getting the assignment for the Peace Corps is already precarious, public support for a radical cause might be just enough to tip the scales against him. Also, older now, able to see things more in the round, he is not entirely convinced the students are taking the right steps.

But at the last second, impulsively he signs the statement. The ad comes out and suddenly he is deluged with phone calls from dozens of people, many of them people he barely knows, saying they knew all along they could count on him. He himself had not been so sure. A psychiatrist he is sent to see as part of his security clearance talks to him only briefly before concluding, "You have moved . . . from missionary to teacher. When you were young and fanatical you thought you could persuade people by the force of reason and conviction, but now you have become infinitely patient. You know that things take time. The frenzy of your youth has given way to the patience of maturity. . . . You're a happy, well-adjusted man. . . . Have a good voyage" (p. 44).

Harris begins to parallel his experiences with the experiences of a character in a developing novel: "As I see it, if things go right, the events of this Phase are producing a plot. Harris the Young Man we have met. We know something about him from his security interrogation. By the skin of his teeth he will be cleared by the FBI and go forth to visit the Peace Corps in far parts of the world. Whom does this middle-aged man meet there? Why, he meets young men and women who are exactly like what he was when he was young. He knows them. They think he is an over-age meddler, arch reactionary, and Establishment conservative—precisely the view he took when he was 21 of men 42" (p. 51).

In the second part of the book, the trip to Africa, the plot goes as predictably and inevitably as a novel possibly could. He is indeed distrusted at first, but when he snubs the ambassador and takes off into the bush with the volunteers, he wins them over to trusting him. The "risks" he interviews are just such as the liberal novelist would have created. One boy noted for his eccentric behavior, it turns out, had with phenomenal skill got through Peace Corps training without anyone realizing he was almost totally blind. Here we find him in town, having started up a school to train blind children. Another couple have outraged previous investigators, as they seemed to be getting rich and fat on their assignment; but when Harris visits them, he finds a pair of pragmatic old farmers who—as in Harris's familiar axiom—thought they could teach best by showing, not telling. So they had first of all started a fantastically successful flourishing farm of their own. As dumb-founded villagers one by one got up the courage to ask them what magic they used, they quickly showed them all the efficient, modern ways of operating a small holding, and little by little the entire area was turning into a lush and productive garden. The farmer hinted to them how they could set up a producers' co-op, and they began selling their produce profitably in near-by villages. He had at first kept all their books, but now was hinting to them that he might be cheating them, and so they were getting interested in learning how to keep their own books.

There is some similar story to be told about each "risk" Harris meets. He has by now made the connection between the Free Speech demonstrators at Berkeley and the Peace Corps "risks" in Kongohno—youthful idealism with impatience but sure instinct cutting through what is negative in the entrenched culture and striving for the good in the most direct possible way. Harris on the one hand knows that life is not that simple, but on the other, vows from now on, without thought, without philosophizing or rationalizing, to adopt instantly on any occasion the radical-left position.

XI *"The Cloud of Self-Indulgence"*

Having said that these books are readable, entertaining, revealing in interesting ways, I must add that in the life of a novelist, which is what Harris preeminently is, they constitute a sort of marking time. He writes about himself, for instance, in 1963, making "several starts at novels and plays,"[5] and finally turning to autobiography. I have tried to suggest in this chapter some of the reasons Harris may have needed to make this turn inward, before recovering—still perhaps somewhat shakily—with *The Goy*.

Jonathan Yardley, in an unusually perceptive review of *The Goy*, said, "The trouble with Mark Harris is that he can't shake Mark Harris. In other guises, notably in three splendid 1950's Henry Wiggen baseball novels . . . he is a funny, perceptive, moving writer. But when an autobiographical or self-analytical impulse strikes him, he descends into a curious blend of whining self-flagellation and intellectual chest-thumping. He has been that way for a decade. . . . 'The Goy' suggests that the cloud of self-indulgence is beginning to lift, but it still hovers."[6]

Perhaps it is a sign of clearing weather that *Killing Everybody*, Harris's most recent novel, is his least autobiographical work so far.

CHAPTER 8

"The Work Itself Is Experience": Mark Harris as Novelist

H ARRIS'S shorter works are plentiful, readable, but minor. At any rate, an examination of them does not in any way extend our study (except, of course, for those in which he directly discusses his own writing), and so will not be attempted here. The short stories are charming, but rather slight. The ideas in his articles generally are spin-offs of ideas in his novels, and where they are not, as in his many occasional pieces, they are not relevant to his writing. By his "writing" I mean his novels. The novel is the form in which, year in and year out, he has been able to tell us all he knows. Next to the novels in importance are his many autobiographical writings, but even these are mainly interesting as they bear on his novels. As we have seen, his novels are frequently "disguised" autobiography. This is no doubt a statement which could be made about most novelists. But Harris has not merely used his life as raw material. He has made the process itself of forming life into art his subject. *The Southpaw* is the story of a young man getting rid of his "greenness." It is also the story of a young novelist learning how to write a novel. What he happens to be writing the novel about is his own life. *Wake Up, Stupid* looks at this process from an earlier stage. While we often see Henry Wiggen in the very act of writing ("That's it. Those are the folks and also the end of the chapter. Holly says try and write up 1 thing and 1 thing only in every chapter and don't be wandering all over the lot, and then, when the subject is covered, break it off and begin another"[1]), what we are presented with in *Wake Up, Stupid* are the documents and experiences *from which* Lee Youngdahl can construct his novel. Writing his letters—in Samuel Richardson's phrase—"to the moment," he must discover as he goes what his theme is, who his heroes are, which lines the action will take.

This is sleight-of-hand, naturally. Harris only pretends to be paring his nails; actually all is presorted, presifted. It is fiction; the appearance of fact. But still, it is fact caught at such an odd moment, in such seeming undress, that careless readers have been fooled by it, have seen no order, but only a haphazard collection of comic or burlesque characters, still waiting for the shaping hand of art.[2]

But with *Twentyone Twice* Harris pushed the process all the way back to actual facts. It is true that even these facts have been sifted and sorted, shaped like and given the themes of the novels. But he has gone too far with his experiment; there has been diminution. Translating life into fiction, poetry was created; but in translating fiction backwards into life, in Frost's phrase, "poetry" is that which has been lost.

I do not mean to be stressing the negative aspects of Harris's experimenting. It seems to me he is often most interesting just where he is playing most dangerously, perhaps, with the nexus between art and life. I have already mentioned *The Southpaw* and *Wake Up, Stupid* in this connection, and they are two of his best books. His other two best books, *Something About a Soldier* and *Killing Everybody*, also deal, at one level, with the problem of converting autobiography into fiction. In the first, Harris takes his youthful experience quite directly, but by placing it against a wide historical background, allegoricizes it, lifts it into fable. It is the technique of one of Harris's favorite books, *The Education of Henry Adams*. In *Killing Everybody*, he has taken an opposite tack: fragmenting himself into the characters, the structure, the language, he has seemingly abandoned all autobiography. And yet here is the clearest statement of his theme thus far. Harris's own daydreams of "killing people left and right," the irritation and frustration of the writer seeing the world no better for all his writing, have gone directly into Brown's equally frustrated daydreams, as he slowly—in fantasy—crushes Stanley Krannick under the wheels of his car. But from there this dream, merely floating in the air, filters down to Berberick somehow, who *acts*, who does crush to death the Stanley Krannicks of the world. Harris has come out the other side, from a theory of converting life into fiction to a theory that fiction is ultimately converted again into life—"poets are the unacknowledged legislators of the world"—but converted back into a better than real life, one that has gone through the ordering process of art.

I *Final Assessment*

If my book is properly written, it has all been an assessment. Certain things, however, are very difficult to get across in a written analysis of a writer. Luckily, these are the things which are most readily apparent to a reader of the actual books. I am speaking first of all of Harris's comedy, which I have scarcely said a word about, though it is one of his major virtues. And next I mean the amazing variety of his characters, which I have touched upon but not really done sufficient justice. Even the most minor characters, I find, stick in my mind with tenacity. I think, for example, of Sid Goldman, the Jewish outfielder on the New York Mammoths. He appears only in a few brief scenes, yet everything about him is right. I would recognize him if I saw him. Joleen's father in *Something About a Soldier* is another.

And I like very subtle things Harris does in characterization, so subtle I am not sure if I can even explain them. For example, the young policeman in *Killing Everybody*, Officer Phelps, has just been told by Brown that Junie (a boyhood friend) was killed in the war. He is shocked, and when he meets Luella, Junie's mother, a short while later, he begins awkwardly trying to express his feelings to her:

> "Junie's in Asia," Luella said.
> Officer Phelps glanced at Brown. In Asia? What was this?
> "That's how Luella prefers to put it," said Brown, "when she's under a certain strain, as she is tonight."[3]

What strikes me as fine here is the young man's being just a bit slow on the uptake, when a more experienced person would have read the situation in an instant and not given anything away in his expression. Harris creates this kind of effect often.

At any rate, the characters, the humor, the "story," these are positive virtues which readers respond to at once. What a study like mine *can* deal with, and what I have stressed, is what, by and large, readers (if I can judge by the reviewers) have missed almost completely. That is the absolute control Harris has over every part of his story, each least echo contributing to what he is writing about. His books are deceptively easy to follow, so readable that readers are lulled into reading them for the jokes, the characters, and then putting them aside and forgetting them. I hope I have shown they are better than that, deserving (and rewarding) more careful reading, for they are carefully composed. Harris is not a deep thinker; he is an artist. This does not mean his works are devoid of ideas, only that the ideas have no great originality in them. Wars will end when young men stop fighting them; the individual is worth more than the Society; money is quickly spent, fame quickly forgotten; in the end your only satisfaction is to know you have acted with integrity. These things need to be said. We cannot quite call them truisms if no one is practicing them. And no doubt there is something liberating in his courage to push his ideas to extremes—in his saying, if they are right, they are always right, whatever the consequences. In a letter to the present writer, Harris said, "I think my work is meaningful, and may profit the world by its being somewhat understood. Katherine Anne Porter says something somewhere about adding one iota to the enlightenment of the world." This is fair, I think, just the right emphasis.

But if the purposes of art are to instruct and delight, it is the second purpose I have been most concerned with. Harris, for all the surface differences, is a writer in the tradition of Henry James, which is to say "the sermon and the proclamation" are not the important thing, but rather "how well you write, how truly." My delight in reading Harris is in my apprehension of the ways he has sought to embody his ideas, of his continual invention and exploration of ways to say, finally, all he knows, and of the human truth he has so often captured along the way. In the letter just referred to, he concluded, "If my work has given you pleasure I am pleased."[4]

Notes and References

Preface

1. Henry Sylvester, "Touching All Bases," *New York Times Book Review* (April 12, 1953), p. 4.
2. Mark Harris's autobiography, *Best Father Ever Invented* (New York, 1976), appeared in print too late to be included in my study. It does not, however, contain material which would cause me to alter any of my interpretations or evaluations of his work as a whole. On the contrary, I was gratified to see how often it confirmed what were on my part educated guesses.

Chapter One

1. John Enck, "Mark Harris: An Interview," *Wisconsin Studies in Contemporary Literature*, 6, No. 1 (Spring-Summer 1965), p. 23.
2. E.g., in *Twentyone Twice: A Journal* (Boston, 1966), p. 18, or p. 57.
3. "Mark Harris: An Interview," pp. 24 - 25.
4. It is curious and perhaps significant that years later Harris was to claim that the theme of the novel was "the loss of Jewish Identity" (*Friedman & Son* [New York, 1963], pp. 29 - 30). My own analysis of the novel (see chapter four below) does not support this.
5. Harris mentions this event twice in his writing: once in the preface to the Charter Books edition of *The Southpaw*, again in *Twentyone Twice*, p. 249.
6. *Friedman & Son*, p. 24.
7. E.g., in *Twentyone Twice*, pp. 17 - 18.
8. *Ibid.*, p. 22.
9. "Easy Does It Not," in *The Living Novel: A Symposium*, ed. Granville Hicks (New York, 1957), pp. 108 - 109.
10. *Twentyone Twice*, p. 30.
11. Introduction to *City of Discontent* (Indianapolis, 1963).
12. *Twentyone Twice*, pp. 3, 11. Harris has admitted to me (Letter to Norman Lavers, May 26, 1977) that the 11,000 figure is a considerable exaggeration. My point remains, however.
13. "Mark Harris: An Interview," p. 26.
14. "Easy Does It Not," p. 117.

15. William Brinkley, "Don't Go Near the Water," *Life* (July 2, 1956), pp. 110 - 24.

16. "Easy Does It Not," p. 117.

17. *Ibid.*, p. 111.

18. "Mark Harris: An Interview," p. 17.

19. *Ibid.*, p. 19 - 20.

20. *Twentyone Twice*, p. 17.

21. "Mark Harris: An Interview," p. 22 - 23.

Chapter Two

1. *Trumpet to the World* (New York, 1946). Parenthetical page references are to this edition.

2. See Harris's own very sarcastic plot summary of *Trumpet to the World* in "How to Write," in *Afterwords: Novelists on Their Novels*, pp. 75 - 77.

3. *City of Discontent* (Indianapolis: Charter Books, 1963), unpaged introduction. Parenthetical page references are to this edition.

4. Because of the fundamentalist religious position Bryan took in the famous "monkey trials" we tend to think of him today as a conservative, but politically and economically he was extremely liberal, a pacifist, and leader of the Populists, a group which, around the turn of the century, attempted to institute a number of Socialist reforms.

5. George Babbitt, the main character in Sinclair Lewis's novel *Babbitt* (1922), became a byword for the narrow and provincial small-town American.

6. *Twentyone Twice*, p. 211.

Chapter Three

1. *The Southpaw* (Indianapolis: Charter Books, 1963), unpaged introduction. Parenthetical page references are to this edition.

2. "Mark Harris: An Interview," p. 19.

3. *Bang the Drum Slowly* (New York, 1956), pp. 22, 38.

4. "Mark Harris: An Interview," p. 22.

5. He told me one day that he had seen a little neighbor girl coming home tightly clutching a loaf of bread. Her mother shouted out the window at her, "Don't wreck the bread." He got a kick out of that. A brief unsigned review of *The Southpaw* in *New Yorker* (May 23, 1953, p. 133), however, questions whether the language derives from life. "His prose derives from classic Lardner locution and is therefore affectedly literary where it is intended to be most authentic. . . . These are surely echoes of the American vernacular of a generation or so before Henry, who was born in 1931."

6. Thucydides (471 - 400 B.C.), the great Greek historian, while writing about actual battles, felt he was at liberty to invent the speeches the

generals must have made to their men. He made these speeches models of high rhetorical skill.

7. "Echoing Ring," unsigned review of *Bang the Drum Slowly*, in *Time* (March 19, 1956), p. 112.

8. "Mark Harris: An Interview, p. 20.

9. *Ibid.*

10. "Easy Does It Not," p. 111.

11. *Bang the Drum Slowly* (New York, 1956). Subsequent page references are to this edition.

12. See Robert Daley, "Henry Was a Southpaw," *New York Times Book Review* (March 18, 1956), p. 5, for a review which typically misses all of Harris's intentions. E.g.: "The actual pennant race is a persistent intrusion."

13. "Mark Harris: An Interview," p. 21.

14. "Easy Does It Not," p. 111.

15. *A Ticket for A Seamstitch* (New York, 1957). Subsequent page references are to this edition.

Chapter Four

1. Granville Hicks also called it his "favorite" of Harris's books ("Eye on the Peace Corps," *Saturday Review* [October 8, 1966], p. 95).

2. *Something About a Soldier* (New York, 1957). All parenthetical page references are to this edition. Harris himself was in the army a good deal longer than "one hundred and twenty-one days," entering January 12, 1943, and being discharged April 7, 1944 ("How to Write," in *Afterwords: Novelists on Their Novels*, p. 66).

3. As I have already mentioned, the fullest account of the actual events underlying the novel is to be found in "How to Write," in *Afterwords: Novelists on Their Novels*, pp. 65 - 79. The principal changes Harris has made have been to reduce the time period and simplify and collapse some of his activities during that period. Most of the characters were at least suggested by actual persons. Harris did not, however, find out what became of the men in his platoon once they went overseas. For other biographical information relevant to this novel: Harris discusses his youthful experiences in the Young Republicans Club campaigning against Roosevelt, in *Mark the Glove Boy, or, The Last Days of Richard Nixon* (New York, 1964), pp. 15 - 16. In the same book, he mentions his close boyhood friend and schoolmate, Norman Apell (to whom *Trumpet to the World* was dedicated), who was killed in Normandy. In the introduction to *Friedman & Son*, Harris reports Norman Mailer's asking him "whether the boy in my book was really I—whether my IQ ran off the charts like that. I said No." Pp. 26 - 27.

4. *The Southpaw* (Indianapolis: Charter Books, 1963), from the unpaged introduction.

5. *Ibid.*, p. 118ff.
6. *Ibid.*, p. 89.

Chapter Five

1. The novel went through three printings in three months (July, August, and September 1959). Harris reports in the introduction to *Friedman & Son* the numerous honors and awards he received following publication of the work (see my discussion of this in chapter seven below).

2. *The Southpaw* was presented to us in the form of a book written by Henry, therefore once more cutting out the middleman, since there is no physical difference between real and fictional autobiography. But the actions were still mediated through an author, even though the author (Henry) was fictional. In *Wake Up, Stupid* there is no putative author, only a chronological gathering of the discrete documents, the letters.

3. *Mark the Glove Boy*, p. 1.

4. *Wake Up, Stupid* (New York, 1959). All parenthetical page references are to this edition.

5. The Aristotelian critical principle of the poet using general, the historian particular truth, was frequently quoted in eighteenth-century Neo-classical literature (see, e.g., *Joseph Andrews*, Bk. III, Chap. 1), and thus fits into the eighteenth-century character of *Wake Up, Stupid* (see section V below).

6. Paul Purdy is no doubt based to an extent on Harris's longtime friend at San Francisco State, Herbert Blau, a founder-director of the well-known San Francisco Actor's Workshop and (briefly) a co-director at the Lincoln Center for the Performing Arts in New York. Paul is, to begin with, nearly an anagram of Blau, and when, a few years after this novel was written, Harris actually wrote a play (*Friedman & Son*), it was at Blau's theater that it was staged.

7. Harris's prescience was considerable: "Playhouse 90, the very television program I thought I had bitterly attacked in [*Wake Up, Stupid*], paid me $7,500 upon my promise to convert the book to script, gilding the bargain by paying my expenses to New York" (*Friedman & Son*, p. 14). The deal finally fell through when the television producer told Harris he could understand the script "intellectually" but doubted that an audience could. "You can't do a show," he said, "that only you and one fine leading actor can understand" (*Friedman & Son*, pp. 22 - 23).

8. *The Goy* (New York, 1970). All parenthetical page references are to this edition.

9. If we allow for the exaggerations of fiction, we see the close application here to Harris himself. A decade before, "all that had been on my mind I had discharged in a novel, *Wake Up, Stupid*, published in July, and so successful in its way that it was soon to carry me beyond accustomed comforts" (*Friedman & Son*, p. 13). As this statement seems to confess, not

only Lee's experiences with commercial literature, but much of his restlessness as well is autobiographical. But what is particularly interesting is that after the considerable success of that novel, Harris did indeed put aside his "disguise," for the next ten years writing direct autobiography (*Mark the Glove Boy, Twentyone Twice*, and beginning his autobiography, *Best Father Ever Invented*), and the autobiographical play *Friedman & Son*, with its lengthy autobiographical introduction. *The Goy* itself is obviously a very personal document, but it is significant that the disguise—i.e., the indirection of fiction—is back in place.

Chapter Six

1. *City of Discontent* (Indianapolis: Charter Books, 1962), from the unpaged introduction.

2. *Twentyone Twice*, p. 71.

3. *Killing Everybody* (New York, 1973). All parenthetical page references are to this edition.

4. In 1965 Harris met Congressman Don Clausen of California, who was sitting across from him in an airplane. "He is a burly insurance man. He wears Western boots, and his wife reads *Redbook*." "I urged him to pass a law regulating the use of firearms, but he said that we have too many regulations. 'Remember Prohibition,' he said. He added, 'That's the price of a free society, Buddy,' warning me that there are sections of Washington, D.C., where I dare not go without a gun. He knew not to say it was the Negro section he was talking about—that's out this year" (*Twentyone Twice*, pp. 158, 161).

5. Harris speaks of his own daydreams in which he finds himself "killing people left and right" (*Twentyone Twice*, p. 86).

6. Here we see clearly his relationship with all those other Harris characters who must keep their hand in every day.

7. Usually, in Harris's works, only the bad characters are careless with words. But Luella is an example of a special executive type who respects and knows how to make use of the writers, the "dreamers." This relationship between Brown and Luella is obviously based on Harris's own relationship with Sargent Shriver when Harris did a Peace Corps assignment for him: "No doubt he is one of those fantastically good administrators. . . . He can keep the end in mind while manipulating the means. He never deceives *himself*. Above all, I'd guess, he can be casual about language, not worry about it, say approximately or roughly what he means, getting his idea across without worrying too much about grace or precision, keeping it loose and general, so that it will have the right effect upon whoever he's dealing with at the moment. Such a man then speaks with power and confidence, and transmits and communicates confidence to others, because, unlike me, he's not forever worrying about the right phrase. . . . And yet he values the man of style, and sees the finally essen-

tial uses of grace or precision. He is a front for all dreamers, giving confidence to the antidreamers because he doesn't himself appear to be a dreamer" (*Twentyone Twice*, pp. 14 - 15).

8. *Twentyone Twice*, pp. 178 - 79.

9. See, for example, his vitriolic and controversial attack in "The Last Article," *New York Times Magazine* (October 6, 1974), pp. 20ff, and also his savage comments in *Mark the Glove Boy*, pp. 48 - 49.

Chapter Seven

1. *Friedman & Son* (New York, 1963). All parenthetical page references are to this edition.

2. *Mark the Glove Boy* (New York, 1964). All parenthetical page references are to this edition.

3. "Voters' Choice Between 'Bread and Butter' Mr. Brown, 'Blue Hot' Mr. Nixon," *Life* (October 19, 1962), pp. 48 - 49.

4. *Twentyone Twice* (Boston, 1966). All parenthetical page references are to this edition.

5. *Twentyone Twice*, p. 5.

6. "Dr. Westrum's Search for Identity," *New York Times Book Review* (October 18, 1970), p. 50.

Chapter Eight

1. *The Southpaw* (Indianapolis: Charter Books, 1963), p. 18.

2. See, for example, the reviews by Carlos Baker, "The Wires Burn and the Mail Flies Hot and Heavy," *New York Times Book Review* (July 19, 1957), pp. 4 - 5, and Granville Hicks, "Portrait of a Nonconformist," *Saturday Review* (July 18, 1959), p. 13.

3. *Killing Everybody*, pp. 28 - 29.

4. Letter to Norman Lavers, March 23, 1975.

Selected Bibliography

PRIMARY SOURCES

The list of primary sources included here is based on a bibliography kindly sent to me by Mark Harris. I have arranged the works in chronological order of publication.

1. Novels

Trumpet to the World. New York: Reynal & Hitchcock, 1946.
City of Discontent. Indianapolis: Bobbs-Merrill, 1952. The reprint by Indianapolis: Charter Books in 1962 contains an autobiographical introduction.
The Southpaw. Indianapolis: Bobbs-Merrill, 1953. The reprint by Indianapolis: Charter Books in 1963 contains an autobiographical introduction.
Bang the Drum Slowly. New York: Knopf, 1956. Most recently reprinted by New York: Dell, 1973.
A Ticket for a Seamstitch. New York: Knopf, 1957.
Something About a Soldier. New York: Macmillan, 1957. Various reprints.
Wake Up, Stupid. New York: Knopf, 1959; London: André Deutsch, 1959.
The Goy. New York: Dial, 1970.
Killing Everybody. New York: Dial, 1973.

2. Autobiography

Mark the Glove Boy, or, The Last Days of Richard Nixon. New York: Macmillan, 1964. Reissued by Curtis Books, 1972, with an Afterword by the author.
Twentyone Twice: A Journal. Boston: Little, Brown, 1966.
Best Father Ever Invented. New York: Dial, 1976.

3. Drama

Friedman & Son. New York: Macmillan, 1963.
Bang the Drum Slowly. A screenplay.

4. Anthology

Selected Poems of Vachel Lindsay. New York: Macmillan, 1963.

5. Short Stories

"Carmelita's Education for Living," *Esquire* (October 1957), pp. 84 - 85.
"Conversation on Southern Honshu," *The North Dakota Quarterly* (Summer 1959), pp. 62 - 65.
"The Self-Made Brain Surgeon," *The Noble Savage* (March 1960); reprinted in *The Best Short Stories: 1961*, ed. Martha Foley and David Burnett. Boston: Houghton Mifflin, 1961, pp. 152 - 67; also in *How We Live*, ed. Rust Hills. New York: Macmillan, 1968.
"At Prayerbook Cross," *Cimarron Review*, No. 6 (December 1968), pp. 6 - 13.

6. Interview

"Mark Harris: An Interview" (by John Enck), *Wisconsin Studies in Contemporary Literature*, 6, No. 1 (Spring-Summer 1965), pp. 15 - 26.

7. Articles and Essays

"This is Baseball's Mediocre Age," *New York Times Magazine* (August 16, 1953), pp. 20ff.
"The Man Who Hits Too Many Home Runs" (on Dick Stuart), *Life* (September 2, 1957), pp. 85ff.
"Easy Does It Not," in *The Living Novel*, ed. Granville Hicks. New York: Macmillan, 1957, pp. 106 - 19.
"Ladies' Day at the Game," *Mademoiselle* (May 1957), pp. 128 - 29.
"Home Is Where We Backed Into," *Nation* (November 1, 1958), pp. 322 - 24.
"The Well-Behaved Fulbright," *New Republic* (February 17, 1958), pp. 16 - 17.
"Old Enough to Know, Young Enough to Care" (interviews of Frost and Sandburg), *Life* (December 1, 1961), pp. 101ff.
"Voter's Choice Between 'Bread and Butter' Mr. Brown, 'Blue Hot' Mr. Nixon," *Life* (October 19, 1962), pp. 48 - 49.
"One American Woman: A Speculation upon Disbelief" (on Marilyn Monroe), in *The Potential of Woman*, ed. Farber and Wilson. New York: McGraw-Hill, 1963, pp. 231 - 40. Reprinted elsewhere.
"On Stage in San Francisco," *Holiday* (October 1965), pp. 180ff.
"How to Write," in *Afterwords: Novelists on Their Novels*, ed. Thomas McCormack. New York: Harper & Row, 1969, pp. 65 - 79.
"Maybe What Baseball Needs Is a Henry David Thoreau," *New York Times Magazine* (May 4, 1969), pp. 66ff.

"Teaching is a Form of Loving," *Psychology Today* (September 1973), p. 59.

"Nixon: A Type to Remember," *The Nation* (August 31, 1974), pp. 134 - 37.

"The Last Article," *New York Times Magazine* (October 6, 1974), pp. 20ff.

Various other essays, reviews, and occasional pieces have appeared in *American Journal, The American Scholar, Arts in Society, The Atlantic Monthly, Book Week, Commentary, Genesis West, Harper's Bazaar, Modern Fiction Studies, The New York Times Book Review, Saturday Review*.

SECONDARY SOURCES

ANONYMOUS. "Echoing Ring," *Time* (March 19, 1956), pp. 110 - 11. A generally positive review of *Bang the Drum Slowly*, but notes that "his characters all talk alike," and so the language, while true, can seem monotonous. Feels Harris's "major success lies in stirring up memories of Ring Lardner."

BAKER, CARLOS. "The Wires Burn and the Mail Flies Hot and Heavy," *New York Times Book Review* (July 19, 1959), pp. 4 - 5. Total misunderstanding of *Wake Up, Stupid*. He feels it is a funny comedy of character which has no plot or meaning. He feels Harris gets a lot of mileage out of the situations, but ultimately falls into low-grade farce.

BROOKS, JOHN. "A Ward Case of Innocence," *New York Times Book Review* (October 27, 1957), pp. 5ff. A typical, total misreading of *Something About a Soldier*. Implies that if Jacob had been a bit more mature and sensible, he would have gone off to war as he was supposed to.

DAYLE, ROBERT. "Henry Was a Southpaw," *New York Times Book Review* (March 18, 1956), p. 5. A typical misreading of the intentions of a Harris novel. He feels that *Bang the Drum Slowly*, "when it sticks to its characters and baseball background" makes wonderful reading, "but the pennant race is a persistent intrusion."

HICKS, GRANVILLE. "Eye on the Peace Corps," *Saturday Review* (October 8, 1966), pp. 95 - 96. A sensitive reading of *Twentyone Twice*. Hicks mentions, just by the way, that *Something About a Soldier* is his favorite Harris work.

————. "Portrait of a Nonconformist," *Saturday Review* (July 18, 1959), p. 13. Sees a pattern of nonconformist heroes in all of Harris's novels. Finds *Wake Up, Stupid* an entertaining book, but serious too—but does not really follow the book, thinks it is unstructured and full of loose ends.

SYLVESTER, HENRY. "Touching All Bases," *New York Times Book Review* (April 12, 1953), p. 4. Review of *The Southpaw*, praises it as "distinguished and unusual book," but bemoans the bad "flaw" of its containing anti - Korean War sentiments.

WALBRIDGE, EARLE. "Mark Harris," *Wilson Library Bulletin*, 30, X (June 1959), p. 716. A biographical sketch.

YARDLEY, JONATHAN. "Dr. Westrum's Search for Identity," *New York Times Book Review* (October 18, 1970), pp. 50 - 51. An unusually perceptive, if rather negative, review of *The Goy*. Rightly sees the decade of autobiographical writing as symptomatic of an artistic crisis in Harris's life, and sees *The Goy* as the first, rather shaky, sign that Harris may be pulling out of it.

Index

(The works of Harris are listed under his name)

151